Admiration of Love

Volume 1

ALAN HINES

Order this book online at www.trafford.com
or email orders@trafford.com

Most Trafford titles are also available at major online book retailers.

Print information available on the last page.

ISBN: 978-1-6987-0703-7 (sc)
ISBN: 978-1-6987-0702-0 (e)

Trafford rev. 04/24/2021

Trafford
PUBLISHING® www.trafford.com
North America & international
toll-free: 844-688-6899 (USA & Canada)
fax: 812 355 4082

BOOKS OF POETRY ALREADY PUBLISHED BY ALAN HINES,

1. Reflections of Love
2. Thug Poetry Volume 1
3. The Words I Spoke
4. Joyce
5. Constant Visions
6. Red Ink of Blood
7. Beauty of Love
8. Reflections of Love Volume 2
9. Reflections of Love Volume 3
10. True Love Poetry
11. Visionary.
12. Love Volume 1
13. This is Love
14. This Is Love Volume 2
15. This Is Love Volume 3
16. Garden of Love
17. Reflections of Love Volume 4
18. Reflections of Love Volume 5
19. Reflections of Love Volume 6
20. Reflections of Love Volume 7
21. Reflections of Love Volume 8
22. Reflections of Love Volume 9
23. Reflections of Love Volume 10
24. Godly Tendecies
25. Permanemt Blood Stain Volume 1
26. Permanemt Blood Stain Volume 2

Urban Novel already published by Alan Hines,

1. Book Writer
2. Queen of Queens
3. Lost in a Poet Storm

Upcoming books of poetry by Alan Hines,

1. Reflections of Love Volume 3
2. This is Love (Volume 1, 2, and 3)
3. Founded Love (Volume 1, 2, and 3)
4. True Love (Volume 1, 2, and 3)
5. Love (Endless Volumes)
6. Tormented Tears (Volume 1, 2, and 3)
7. A Inner Soul That Cried (Volume 1, 2, and 3)
8. Visionary (Endless Volumes)
9. A Seed That Grew (Volume 1, 2, and, 3)
10. The Words I Spoke (Volume 2, and 3)
11. Scriptures (Volume 1, 2, and 3)
12. Revelations (volume 1, 2, and 3)
13. Destiny (Volume 1, 2, and 3)
14. Trials and Tribulations (Volume 1, 2, and 3)
15. 15. IMMORTALITY (Volume 1,2, and 3)
16. 16. My Low Spoken Words (Volume 1, 2, and 3)
17. Beauty Within (Volume 1, 2, and 3)
18. Red Ink of Blood (Volume 1, 2, and 3)
19. Destiny of Light (Jean Hines) (Volume 1, 2, and 3)
20. Deep Within (Volume 1, 2, and 3)
21. Literature (Volume 1, 2, and 3)

22. Silent Mind (Volume 1, 2, and 3)
23. Amor (Volume 1, 2, and 3)
24. Joyce (Volume 1, 2, and 3)
25. Lovely Joyce (Volume 1, 2, and 3)
26. Pink Lady (Volume 1, 2, and 3)
27. Mockingbird Lady (Volume 1, 2, and 3)
28. Godly tendicies (Volume 1, 2, and 3)
29. Enchanting Arrays (Volume 1, 2, and 3)
30. Harmony (Volume 1, 2, and 3)
31. Realism (Volume 1, 2, and 3)
32. Manifested Deep Thoughts (Volume 1, 2, and 3)
33. Poectic Lines of Scrimage (Volume 1, 2, and 3)
34. Garden of Love (Volume 1, 2, and 3)
35. Reflection In The Mirror. (Volume 1, 2, and 3)

UPCOMING NON-FICTION BOOKS BY ALAN HINES,

1. Time Versus Life
2. Timeless Jewels
3. The Essence of Time
4. Memoirs of My Life
5. In my Eyes To See
6. A Prisoner's Black History

UPCOMING URBAN NOVELS BY ALAN HINES,

1. Black Kings
2. Playerlistic
3. The Police
4. Scandalous Scandal

ACKNOWLEDGEMENTS

Heavenly Father thank you for blessing me to live to see
another day; thank you for all your
many blessings which
include me writing and being able
to publish another book.

1. TO BE THERE FOR YOU

Be there for you til the end of time.
Be there for you to ease pressure
make love to your mind.
I'll be there for you as the days turn to night, seasonal
changing of time, blessed to have you as mines.
Be there for you even when souls and Heaven
combine.

I'll be there for you until the end of time.

2. JEWELS OF JOURNEY

Jewels of time.
Timeless.
Jewels of intimacy.
Lovely she.
Lovely as can be.
Lovely as the Dolphins that swin through Seas.
A jewel, a Gem, a Diamond of love, she.

The journey of love.
Journey time find timeless bliss.
I found it I never knew a love like this.
A journey a quest of time conquered, she's the loveliest.

3. A VISION, A DREAM

A vision a dream.
Love as it seems.
Reality of love seen,
as we sail down streams.
My fair lady my queen.
Such a delightful wonderful human being.
A visionary of time, my lady of dreams.

4. NICKNAMED, LOVE

In the name of love.
I nicknamed her love.
She was love.
She is love.
Since birth she loved.

5. UPRISE

Uprise.
Love to forever rise.
To rely.
No tears to cry.
Love undying, undie.
A prize.
To grow, uprise.

6. PROPOSED

Proposed.
The gift of life,
red Rose.
A new beginning to flow.
Love that shall continue to grow.

7. SHE DEVOTED

Her loyalty of love she devoted.
Making potion.
Smoothly coasting.
Floating.
Love tenderness noted.
To me she provided love, life, loyalty,
devoted.

8. LOVE MY WAY

Love my way.
Shine my way.
Forever more stay.

9. SAINT

The saints of time.
The love that came up
to date from Biblical times.
The love that scriptures spoke about,
holy and divine.
She was a latter day saint of time.
The loveliest love of all times.

10. COULDN'T REPLACE

Couldn't replace.
Deface.
Not even just in case.
No second chance as
the whistling winds of times open
and closed gates.
A love I never wanted to escape.
Great.
Could never replace.

11. BLESSED BY THE BEST

Blessed.
Blessed by the best.
Still living but in peace I rest.
Of your love I confess.
I must say I'm truly blessed.

12. ANOINTED BY

Anointed by the Lord.
One accord.
The Lord is the one I worship,
I adore.
As his child I know he loves me more.
Spanish amor.
Wealthy love of riches when times of
life seem poor.
Always there when this cold world
in the Winter maintains opened doors.

Anointed by his blessing oil of love
in which I adore, one accord.

13. DEALINGS

The feeling.
The living.
Bond building.
Living in an environment
of delightful dealings.

14. MONARCH

Her a monarch.
A shining in the dark.
My queen of hearts.
The greatest love thus far.

15. PLEASE PROCEED

Proceed.
Be all you can be.
keep being lovely to me.
Love me.

Proceed to allow our hearts,
and minds to be free.

Proceed on loving, loving me.

16. YOU BE DIVINE

You be the divineness of time.
You be the reason I shine.
You be a victory of mountains I climb.
You be my love of life, life, time.
You be divine.

17. IN

In love.
In desire.

In love.
Enchanting.

In love.
Lovely romancing.

18. COME TO ME

Come to me in your times of need.
I shall share my oxygen mask so we both can breathe.

Come to me in time of despair
knowing I'll always be there.

Come to me with secrets unknown
I'll be strong like a hard rock
of stone.

Come to me in times of need, love indeed,
each others love is all we need.

19. BE

Be mines like shining of days in our lives,
of lifetimes.

Be free, as those released from condensed places
liberty to be.

Be great by the ruler of this world in which
God had to create.

Be my love as an gaurdian angel from up above.

20. A NEW YOU

A new you,
a new me a new us.

A new day new error,
as the beast we continue to crush.

A new beginning with no ending.

A new love gotta be Heavenly from up above.

21. DISTANT LOVERS

We was far from apart.
Together our souls would embark.
She be lovely as a shining star.
A beautiful creature you are.
The howling of love within the full moons
within the night that shine in our heart,
as a light even after dark.
My tree of love, my tree of life you are.
Distant lovers but together our hearts
are ever more joined to never be apart.

22. LIFTING

Lift every voice and gleam.
Let out love be ever more like endless
eternal sleeping dreams.

Let our love be like the harmony of liberty as our
love blow like the winds easy and free.

Let our rejoice be high as the clouded skies.
Love to forever more rely.

23. ADMIRED HER

I'd admire her style her grace.
Love laced.
Lovely in every way.
Love that couldn't be replaced.

24. IMPRESSED

Impressed.
Blessed.
You are the best.
Confess.
Tenderness of heart, mind, flesh.

I'm impressed.

25. SOMEONE

Someone that I predict my future with.
Loves assist.

Someone I can forever share my world lovely girl.

Someone that I can kneel down
with to pray my starlight
of each day.

26. SPRING

Sing.
Spring.
My love thing.
My queen.
My everything.

27. FOR THE PEOPLE

A person for the people.
Treated each one as equal.

A woman of genuine nature.
Love that didn't get greater.

A great mind.
Love all the time.

28. NEST

Caress.
Love fest.
Love nest.
Love without rest.

29. ONE IN

One in the same.
Love gained.

We are as one.
Stunning as it comes.

Great.
Great like the five lakes.

30. TO WITHSTAND

To withstand.
Love supplied in demand.
Yes I can.
Lovely and grand.

31. LOVING AS

Loving as a plus.
For your heart and soul I lust.
My everyday crush.
Together as one, us.

32. TO BE LOVED

To be loved.

To be appreciated.

To be cherished.
Love and marriage.

33. THE BREEZE

The breeze of time.
The love is divine.

The changing of days.
My daily parade.

The essence of truth.
Love you.

34. LOVE IS LOVE

Love.
Love is being there in times of
needs, storms, floods.

Love.
Love is a vision of the truth,
thereof.

Love is being by my side
even if it's not physical,
but spiritually there in love.

Love is love.

35. CAN WE

Can we be each others peace.
Watching sunset in the East.

Can we be each others joy.

Can we be each others sunshine;
each others love of a lifetime.

36. WITHOUT SHAME

I love you to the fullest without any regret of shame.
Fame.
I long to be with you simply love hearing your name.
From your wisdom I have alot to gain.
Live forever as love became.
Fame.

37. CONTROLLED

Control my fate.

Controlled my destiny she.

Controlled my love to be, she.

38. IMAGES

Images in the mirror,
love became clearer.

Images time,
spiritually inclined divine.

Images of being great,
lovely as the coming of days.

39. SUCH A FINE

Such a fine specimen of a woman.
Love in abundnace.

Such a talented lady.
Highly appraise thee.

Such a dream girl.
Share my vitality,
share my world.

40. IF SHE

If she was the sun she'd shine brighter than day.

If she was the clouds she'd wash away the rainy days.

If she was the moon our nights would
be enchanting without gloom.

41. ENGAGED, ESCAPADES

Engaged.
Love escapades.
Charades.
Enchanting array.
A product of the environmental
species in which the creator made.

Engaged.
Love escapades.

42. LOVELY DAY

Lovely day.
Lovely one shine my way.
Lovely lady of blue skies within the month of may.

Lovely lady be like a butterfly to take to
the sky after the transformation.
Congratulations.
Love across the nation.

43. TAKE FLIGHT

Take flight.
Be high off scriptures,
high off life.
A delight.
Fly soar like runaway kite.
Be ones shining day, Moonlight night.

Take flight.
Live it up,
enjoy life.

44. LOVE AND

Love and opportunity.
Love and unity.
Love and immunity.

45. I ADMIRE YOU

I admire you.
Love you.
Believe in you.
A dream come true.

46. I LOVE THE

I love the way you make me shine.
I love you as my everyday Valentine.
I love you more within coming of age within time.
I love you, you're the greatest of all times.

47. ATTAIN

Attain.
Love remain.

Give.
Love me for the rest of my years.

Proclaim.
Proclaim me as your fortune,
and fame.

48. YOU BRING

You bring joy, satisfaction.
Love everlasting.

You bring peace,
love to increase.

You bring all the goodness of time,
pleasant memories in mind,
the love of good spirits to intwine.

You bring me to the realization of
affection of the present day and futuristic
time combine.

You bring love to my heart, and mind.

49. YOU MUST

You must be an angel,
loving and aimful.

You must be a Greek Goddess
of the sun love as a champion, you won.

You must be the white sands of time,
lovely at all times, promoted in your prime.

You must be from another planet,
love I can stand it.

50. MOST

Most gracious,
standing ovation.

Most high,
love to rely.

Most adored,
hearts the same as one accord.

51. CRUISE

Cruise.
Subdue.
Remain true.
Love due.
Love unto.

52. UNTIL

Until the stars no longer coincide with the sun,
loving as one.

Until our Earthly flesh is put to rest,
loving at it's best.

Until the spaceships fly away to escape
dismay as the book of Revelations comes to light
in the darkness of day our love will forever stay.

53. LOVE SIGNS

Capricorn perfected, again born.

Cancer, such a great romancer.

Gemini, love together you and I.

54. AT

At peace.

At love.

At clouds.
Love out loud.

55. SOLID LOVE

The love that was solid as a rock.
Stood firm throughout times when others would not.
The love around the clock.
She loved me non-stop.

56. AMAZED, CRAZED

Amazed.
I be your biggest fan crazed.
Freedom for the slaves.
Spiritual could never be man made.
Love poetry to convey.

Amazed.
Please continue to shine my way.

57. IS, WAS

Love she is, was.

Love as being in the world all
alone no animosity of war zones.

Love as an Island alone her and I.

Love she is and was just because
she geniunely loved.

58. LORD OF DREAMS

Lord of dreams.

Lord of lords,
king of kings.

The inventor of life,
to be baptize.
The awakening, the closing of eyes.
Love to depend rely.
Even in hardships of time,
the Lord shall always be by your side.

59. SUDDENLY SHE

Suddenly outta nowhere she came.
Like a shadow in the night she'd follow
me to the land of granted promises, love gained.
Across her heart was my name.
Lovely as the sun the rainbow after the rain.
Lovely as unconditionally kids play joyous games.

Suddenly outta nowhere like a ghost
she appeared she came.
A love as reality placed as an image in a frame..

Suddenly she came.

60. WELL SPENT

Well spent.
Love meant.
Evident.
My lady love,
my womenly prince.

61. RUNNETH

Runneth over.
Never ending love,
never over.
Together growing older.
My life with you as our love
runneth over.

62. SUCH A

Such a special lady.
Love positively, without the probability of maybe.
Lovely lady.

Such a great woman,
love in abundance.

Such an asset to my life,
marry me be my wife.

63. GOD IS MY EVERYTHING

God is my everything.
God is everything.
God is my king of kings.

64. CONJOINED

Conjoined.
Joined.
You be my token of love
as a gem, a diamond,
sapphire, a metal, a bronze coin.

65. KEEP BRINGING

Keep bringing.
Keep singing.

Keep believing.
Keep striving for acheivement.

66. LIKE THE SHEEP

Like the sheep that followed Christ.
Like reaching Heaven paradise.

Like feeling the cool breeze as we float through time.
Like making love, love to ones mind.

Like being set free through appeals of circumstances.
Like being laced with love romancing.

Like living in a castle as the king.
Like having you by my side as the queen.

67. MORE TO

More to come.
Destine, destiny.

More to live.
Live your life to the fullest of years.

More to earn.
Live and learn.

68. SHE WAS A

She was a saint like Nick.
She was love in the mix.

She's beautiful and stunning.
Love that kept running.

She was the essence of great.
More lovelier day by day.

69. LOVE EFFECT

Love, affection.
Tender caressing.
Loving the beauty of her heart's
core and the attractiveness of her flesh.

Love effect.

70. WE SHALL

In time we shall overcome.
Love there and from.

We shall unite as the sky with the rising of the sun.
We shall be released as love from the East.

As one we shall ever more be.

71. GOOD OMEN

My lover, my best friend.
Love with no end.

My love entanglement.
My love in which
was angelic sent.

My time, my moment.
Loving, omen.

72. REMIND ME OF

You remind me of a sweet dream.
You remind me of a queen of queens.
You remind me as a eternal light of love that gleams.
You remind me of all the wonderful
things the joy of life brings.

73. LOVE TRUE, UNTO

Love true.
Love unto.
Love you.
Lovely as the sky blue.
Love being near you.
Love simply hearing your voice to.
I do, I do love you.

Love true, unto

74. CLIMB, BUILD

Climb.
Move forward,
no backtracking to rewind.

Build.
Build a fortress of steel.

Make.
Make your time on Earth great.

75. ADDING

In addition,
a plus.
Loving together, us.

Adding with no subtraction.
Love everlasting.

76. A SYMBOL

A symbol of love as an art.
A symbol saving lives as an Ark.
A symbol freedom of love greatness is who
you be who you are.
Shine like a shining star.

77. SHE PROVIDED

She provided love and tranquility to coincide.
An uprise.
A prize.

She provided an everlasting love to never die.

78. SHARE MY LOVE

It's nothing I'd rather do than share my love with you.

Made a change in me love you be.

You came my way, love for you to stay.

Share my love with you.
Female guru.

79. LOVE STRONG

The love we share is strong.
Love carry on.
Love in a pleasurable tone.
Falling deeper in love with you as
time frames continue on.
Love strong.

80. LOVE TO GIVE

Love to give.
Happier within access of New Years.
Love be near.
Loving you here.
Love sincere my dear.

Love to give.

81. AWAIT

Await.
Outdate.
Perfected in every way.
Lovely as the coming of days.

82. ADORE, GALORE

Adore.
Galore.
Wanting, needing you
more and more.
A new beginning the opening of new door.
You love, I love you more.

Adore, galore.

83. LOVE AND GROWTH

Time.

Love.

Growth.....

The seed of knowledge,
loving you the most.

Love overdose.
Forever close.
My friendly ghost.
Love and growth.

84. FOREVER SHINE

In mind.
In time.
Forever be mines.
Forever shine.
Love all the time.

85. LIVE, ALIVE

Alive.
Pleasurable ride.

Live.
Love me for what it's worth,
what it is.

Give.
Continue to give unconditional love throughout years.

86. FEAST, PEACE

Feast.
Love to love, love to never cease.

Peace.
Peace be multiplied throughout
the North, South, West, East.

Obsolete.
Our ex lovers to permanently be deleted.

87. GRANTED

Granted wishes.
Granted time.
Granted love.
Granted peace in mind.

88. STRENGHTEN ME

Strenghten me.
Live within me.
Love me.
Put no one above me.

89. I WANT

I want to be your peace.

I want to be your happiness, bliss.

I wanted to be your good weather, loving whenever.

I want to rejoice and sing as you lift every voice.

90. EMERGED

Emerged.
Love respect and deserve.

Emerged from the bottom to the top
to fly away as chirping love birds.

Emerged as progession of time
to embark within love like dinner love is served.

Emerged.

91. I'D RATHER

I'd rather spend the rest of my life with you.

I'd rather make your dreams come true.

I'd rather for our love affair to be soothing as melodies from a flute.

92. ASPIRING

Aspiring.
Admiring.
Love me without retiring.

93. BELOVETH

Beloveth.
I love it.
Gatherings of festivals,
sisters, brothers, cousins.

Dearly beloveth.
I love it.

Beloveth.
Up above it.

Beloveth.

94. TO THE SKY

To the sky.
To the space.
Love that can't be replace.
Love laced.
Love from coast to coast,
state to state.
Love laced.

95. IT'LL NEVER BE

It'll never be another you.
Never be another her.
Never be another she.
Never be more finer to possess,
at it's best.

It'll never be.

96. US

Us.
We.
Her and I.
She and him.
Love as one to begin.

97. BRING BACK

Bring back the days of yesterday,
as kids we play my first teenage love of yesterday.

Bring back the time of virginity,loving infinite.

Bring back the love that was genuine
before the evil benefits
came to mind to swim.

Bring back the art of love in the
daytime before it got grim.

98. BURNING

Determined.
Yearning.
Learning.
Earning.
Burning.

99. I SEE YOU

I see you as my light.
My shine.
My gleam.

I see you as my only,
as for your love I fiend.

I see you as vision of the fruitful
fruit of truth.

I see you as a heart of love unto.

100. THE POWER OF LOVE

The power of love.
To make me feel love to enhance love floods.

To make me feel great.

To make me feel as a martian from out of space.

Upcoming Urban Fiction Novels

Kidnapping

CHAPTER 1

It was noon time scorching hot summer's day as the sunlight from the sky lit up the streets, the public was tired of blacks being murdered by the police, and a shame of how black on black crime continuous increase.

It was madness in the city streets two unarmed black males were killed by the punk police; one was home from college pulled over at a traffic stop the police shot and killed him in cold blood, the police lied and said that they thought his cell phone was a gun, the victim had no gun no prior arrest, no criminal background; the other black male that was shot was one of their very own, he was an off duty seargent, the white cops walked up to him to search him assuming he was a street thug, as the off duty seargent went to reach for his badge the racist cops shot him three times in the left side of his chest instantly seperating life from death as the four five bullets ripped through his heart he instantly fell to the concrete visualizing stars as he life no longer existed organs torn apart.

People of all colors came together on and every side of town; north, south, east, and even the west. Through the city streets they marched, and protest only in signs and symbols of peace. Hoping the violence would come to an end, that it would cease.

On Madison street people stood on all four corners as if they owned it. They were together as one, White, Blacks, Mexicans, Puerto Ricans, and even a few Arabics were presents; they all wore t-shirts that displayed Black Lives Matter, some were holding up signs that displayed honk you horn if you love Jesus.

Almost each car that rode past the crowds of people honked their horns; some yelled out there windows, "we love you Jesus," as others yelled out there windows loud and clear, "black lives matter."......

Daily around the city meetings were being held in churches, unioun halls, amongst various other places but all on one accord to stop the violence.

Hundreds of protestors peacefully marched up to city hall with picket signs, telling

those at city hall that the violence just gotta stop......

The mayor of the city, and the police commisioner came together and made a statement on the news saying that he, and the Chicago police Department will be doing all they can to decrease the violence in the city streets......

Mysteriously three black teenage girls came up missing, and had been missing for many months; the authorities had no leds to there whereabouts.....

After a innocent twelve year old black girl was killed by stray bullets, her mother was interviewed at the scene of the crime by the channel 9 news......

Running down her face drowning tears of sorrow knowing that her twelve year old daughter was dead wouldn't be here to live to see another day tomorrow.

She cried out on the channel 9 news in front of the camera for people stop the violence.

The grieving mother told the news,"the police don't give a fuck about us, if they killing our young black males, what makes everybody think they give a fuck about finding those missing girls. It wouldn't surprise me if they never find the bitch that killed my little girl."

Oh how her angry harsh words was so true.

The authorities searched and searched, did a thorough investigation, but no killer was found and charged with the murder of twelve year old Shante Smith.....

CHAPTER 2

"The niggas off the low-end been eating real good, them niggas been performing," Kuda said. "They been kidnapping niggas, they be trying to grab any nigga getting some real bread," Big Shorty said. "Awwww that's how them niggas been eating like that," Kuda said. "What they do is they kidnapp a nigga for a healthy ransom, or rob a nigga for some weight, and then whatever they get they invest it in buying more weight, flooding the low end with hella narcotics," Big Shorty said. "That's smart," Kuda said.....

Early one sunday morning Kuda sat in the park across the street,slightly up the block from where the shorties slang his rocks.

Big Shorty walked up to Kuda, as Kuda set fire to a Newport long, Kuda took a long pull off the square, as Big Shorty could see, and feel a sense of distress.....

"Man Big Shorty we got to hit us a lick, rob a nigga, kidnapp a nigga or something," Kuda said. "Your joint doing pretty good, why you wanna take some other nigga shit," Big Shorty said. "My joint only sell like a stack or two a day, it take me two or three days to scrap up the money to re-copp to go get another four and a baby, you feel me," Kuda said. "But you still eating alot of these niggas out here broke ass hell,"

Big Shorty said, "True, but look at the niggas off the low end they got joints selling 10 or 20 thousand a day, some of them even got two or three joints, selling weight and robbing niggas all at the same damn time, that's what I call getting money," Kuda said.....

Big Shorty remained silent for a brief moment knowing that Kuda was speaking the truth.....

"But Kuda it's so much chaotic madness, that comes along with sticking up. Them niggas off the low-end in constant danger," Big Shorty said. "I'm already in constant danger for all the shootings I've been doing over the years, representing the business for the hood, I deserve to be eating good, fuck the dumb shit I gotta hit me a lick," Kuda said.

Big Shorty remained silent again for a brief moment realizing the realization of what Kuda was talking about.....

Kuda joint started to get sweating more by the police because all ths shooting, that was going on in the area. It was hard for Kuda to work because of the police sweating his joint, and because the hood was in war.

Now Kuda really knew he had to hit a lick to get some fast cash.....

More and more Kuda talked to Big shorty about hitting a lick.....

Kuda and Big Shorty ended up getting up with a few guys from the hood that was highly interested in kicking in some doors, and taking another nigga shit.....

A few guys from the hood knew of a few houses on the other side of town where niggas was holding drugs and money at.

Kuda, Big Shorty, and the few guys from the hood kicked in a few doors hitting licks. Each lick they came up on several thousands outta each house, which wasn't shit to them because they had to split it five ways each time.

Kuda was hungry to eat, he was tired of small time nickels and dimes he wanted to do it big.....

One of the guys from the hood that they went on the licks with seen how well

Kuda, and Big Shorty performed when they ran in them houses, and decided to set them up to kidnapp his sister boyfriend. The guy couldn't do it himself because his sister boyfriend knew him, and he didn't want to send nobody else but Kuda, and Big shorty because other people was messy and would fuck shit up.

The guy sister would be the one to set her boyfriend up, she was tired of the nigga he was to cheap, but the nigga had long money.....

They planned on kodnapping him for thirty thousand, splitting it up evenly four ways a piece, therefore each individual would get seventy-five hundred a piece.....

Kuda was charged up, this is the kind of lick he was interested in hitting.....

Two in the morning as the streets lights lit up the sky, Kuda and Big Shorty set in the car parked several cars behind their soon to be victims car.

Kuda took a long hard pull of the last of his Newport long, inhaling, and exhaling

the smoke out of his nose as if it was a blunt filled with loud.

Once Kuda was finish smoking the cigarette he threw the butt out the window.....

Outta nowhere comes this guy sister, and her boyfriend out the door walking down the porch.....

Her and her boyfriend made their way to the back of his car, and started tongue kissing him in which seemed so delightful for the both of them.

As their lips and tongues disconnected he opened his trunk searching for a purse he had bought her.....

As he lift his head up trying to give her, her bag outta nowhere Kuda appeared instantly back hand slapping the shit out of him upping a big ass gun putting it to his stomach. As Big Shorty came from the back putting a gun to his head forcing him inside the trunk, as the girlfriend cried tears pleading with them to stop; she put on a great performance, she should've won a Oscar for.

As the trunk closed she started smiling, glad that they got his ass. But she continued crying and pleading with them to stop just in a case a neighbor was watching.

Kuda drove the victim off in his own car as Big shorty followed Kuda in his car; the girlfriend ranned in the house crying as they pulled off.

Once she made it in the house she called her brother and told him,"they got his bitch ass".....

She left out the house went to her car and drove slowly to the nearest police station which took her approximately twenty minutes.....

She ran inside the police station crying emotional tears, that seemed really, real.

She told the police that her boyfriend was kidnapped, she gave up false identities of the kidnappers.

The police asked why didn't she call immediately after it happen. She told the police that the kidnappers robbed her for her phone and money so she couldn't call, and that she went to two of the neighbors house and they never answered their door bells.....

After finishing the police report she went home sipped some wine, relaxed in a hot bubble bath, thinking of the things she'd do with her seventy five hundred once she had it in her possession.....

Two days passed overlapping into nights; now it was crunch time. Kuda and Big Shorty had made arrangements for the kidnapped victims people to run thirty stacks.

They was supposed to leave the money in a trunk of a car parked near a shopping center that was closed, it was closed because it was the middle of the night, but during the day it would regularly be open.

Before they even made it there with the thirty stacks Kuda, and Big Shorty circled all around the area, there were no police cars or unmarked cars nowhere to be found.

Right before the victims people brought the money, Kuda and Big Shorty watched from a far distance with binoculars as some old lady came, bent down got the keys from under the left back tire as instructed.

As she opened the trunk Kuda, and Big shorty begin cheering, giving each other constant high fives.

She put the money in the trunk and the keys back under the left tire as instructed, and walked away disappearing into the night.

Kuda and Big shorty waited for approximately twenty minutes just to make sure the coast was clear, then they text the chick they had designated to go pick the money up.

She made it there in no time. As she walked up to the car bent down picked up the keys from under the left tire, opened up the passenger door.

As soon as she sat down, before she could even close the door, twenty unmarked cars surrounded her out of nowhere, all she heard was sirens and seen guns upped on her from

every which way. It was impossible for her to get away.....

The police grabbed her by the neck slamming her face to the concrete, cuffed her up, roughed her up a little and put her in the back of one of the police cars.

The police drove her, and the vehicle that the money was in to the police station to further pursue their investigation.....

Kuda, and Big Shorty watched the whole thing through binoculars, shook the fuck up.....

Once the police left Kuda, and Big shorty pulled off confused not knowing what to do.....

Shortly after leaving the seen of the crime Kuda stopped at a nearby pond and threw his cell phone in it. From Big Shorties phone he called his phone carriers hot line, telling them his phone was stoling and had been missing for hours, he had insurance, so they'd definitely replace it. He threw his phone in the pond, because he text the chick that the police just grabbed from his phone, so if the police went through her phone and linked the text back to his phone he could say it wasn't him, that someone stole his phone.....

As they proceeded back driving home they both was worried, wondering if the girl would play fair ball, or switch up like a bitch and snitch.

Kuda was driving as Big Shorty kept looking back every two or three minutes to see if they was being followed by the cops.

"What the fuck, why is you steady looking back for," Kuda asked? "The police might be following us," Big Shorty said. "The police is not following us if the police wanted us we'd already been got. I hope the bitch didn't tell, I know she did," Kuda said.

"Straight up," Big Shorty said.

Once they made it to the police station at first she played like she didn't speak any English.

She was Boricua, Kuda had nicknamed her the thrill seeking Puerto Rican, because she was adventurous loved violence. Even when the police grabbed her and roughed her up, she loved it.

Months prior to her arrest Kuda, and Big Shorty use to fuck her at the same time; she loved two dicks at once she preferred one in the mouth, and another in her pussy at the same time as Kuda, and Big Shorty would choke her and slap her around in the midst of sex.

She was a bad bitch she just got an adrenaline rush off hardcore shit.....

As the police proceeded questioning her even when they went to get her an interpreter she winded up speaking to them in English.

The cops came to find out her name was Maria Rodriguez. She had been to the joint before twice, once for a kidnapping, and the other time for robbery, and was still on parole for the robbery.

She lied and told the cops that someone paid her to go pick up that car, only because they was pulled over by the police for driving with no license, and once the police left they came back to leave an additonal set of keys under the left tire so she could pick the car up since she had license. To assure them that she had no knowledge of a kidnapping.....

The police knew her story was bullshit, so they asked her who didn't have license and sent her to pick the car up for that reason. She told them she couldn't give any names, because she didn't know what was going on.....

The police pleaded with her for hours to give up a name or names, she didn't tell them shit.

They ended up fingerprinting her processing her in and charging her with kidnapping and sending her to the County Jail.

Of course she didn't want to be locked up, but she wasn't worried at all, on her bus ride to the County she'd vision all the pussy she'd be eating once she made it within and started mingling and getting to know the other girls.

After a few days rolled around Kuda, and Big Shorty didn't know what to do with the victim. Normally in a situation like that the individual that had been kidnapped would be put to death since the people got the police involved.

Kuda, and Big Shorty contemplated long and hard about killing the Vic, but decided not to, because if they did they could possibly give Maria a conspiracy to murder, and she could start singing the blues to the police telling them everything.....

After about a week in the middle of the night they dropped the vic off and left him in a abandon building still blindfold and tied up, called his people and the police and told them where to get him from.

Kuda and big Shorty wasn't worried about the vic sicking the police on them; he didn't even never see their faces, they had on masks, and even if he did see their faces he didn't know them or there whereabouts because they were from different sides of town.....

After a few weeks Kuda, and Big Shorty was able to get in touch with Maria, she'd call them collect continously.

Come to find out, she was a down bitch, didn't tell the police shit; they kind of figured she didn't snitch because she knew where Kuda, and Big Shorty lived, and if she would've told the police would've been at their house by now.

Kuda and Big Shorty wanted to bond her out, or atleast put up something on her bond, but she couldn't bond out because she was on parole, she had a parole hold.

Kuda and Big Shorty started sending her money orders constantly to make sure she was straight in there.....

The vic they kidnapped continued dating, fucking around with the chick that set him up to get kidnapped, never in his wildest dreams would he even assume that she was the one that set him up to get kidnapped. Later in life he even ended up getting the bitch pregnant with twins.....

CHAPTER 3

Black lives matter was getting to be an even more major issue.

Peaceful protest even seemed to get violent. The black politicians and even black cops was sick and tired of being sick and tired of all the killing blood spilling of the black population.....

More and more teenage black girls would mysteriously come up missing. More and more gangs were waring harder throughout the city, North, South, East, West.....

The black people begin to have meetings quite often mainly at churches, and Union halls.....

One night they had a meeting to their surprise unnumbered white people, and Latinos showed up to support black lives matter; they wore shirts and buttons displaying all lives matter.

The meeting became slightly hostile as not the blacks or Latinos, the white people started snapping out saying that racism does exist, and they were tired of blacks losing their lives by gun-fire, especially from white-police officers that gets paid from tax-payers money to serve and protect the community, when all along they were causing the deaths and destruction within the community, it so much killing and hate, seemed as if it was no-love, nor unity.....

They allowed this one white lady to approach the front to get on the stage onto the pulpit, to preach the bullshit.....

"If we study our past history blacks were hung, lynched by white mobs, shot down by angry white fire squads, and even killed by the police as the same way today. With the 1900's many white that committed hate crimes against blacks were either investigated by the police, some even were put on trial and as documenting they were liberated of their crimes. History does repeat itself in a way. Now technology is advance and I've seen with my own eyes on video, shown white police killing black men, and even after shown on video surveillance, the officer still gets acquitted of all charges someway somehow.

If a black man kills another black man he'll immediately be placed in prison until trial, and in large unnumbered cases he'll get found guilty. And if a black man kills a white person in most cases that black man will eventually get found guilty, and sentenced to excessive time in prison possibly until he dies of natural causes. That's one of the main problems with the police brutality and unjustified murders of blacks they know they can get away with it because they are the police. What need to happen is that the police need to start getting persecuted and sent to prison for their crimes of hate. Until they start getting convicted of the crimes the madness won't stop," she said.....

As she dropped the mic tears flowed freely from her eyes. Knowing that racism was still alive. Lucifer's legacy of racism and hate wasn't decreasing any, but instead it begin coinciding with his sick enterprise.

Everyone in the church begin clapping, and cheering impending her speech.....

This one lady sat in the back all the way in the corner dressed in black with a veil over her face as if she was going to a funeral; she cried silently of sorrow drowning watery tears that shall forever shed throughout her lifetime of years wishing it never happen, wishing her son was still living, still here.....A few years prior to that date her son was wrongfully shot down, murdered by the nation, better known as the police; the two officers that killed her son did stand trial, and was acquitted of all charges against them of her sons murder.....

Soon as the second individual stepped to the pulpit to voice his opinion, gun shots rang out, five of em, sounding like a canon was outside.....

Everyone in the church got frightened, and then within rage everyone ran out the church, not scared of the gun-fire, but pissed the fuck off.

They ran out the front door in a rage eagerly trying to see who was shooting, and what for.....

As majority of the people had exited the church it was still more rushing out the front door, one woman spotted a guy up the block laid out on the sidewalk.

She yelled out to everyone, "it's somebody down there laid out on the sidewalk."

Everybody rushed to the individual that was laid out.

Come to find out it was a teenage boy that was still breathing, living. He had been shot once in the ass, and once in both of his legs.....so that meeting was officially over for that night.

As they approached him they seen him shot up as blood ran perfusely down the sidewalk he'd repeatidely keep saying, "I can't believe that pussy ass nigga shot me;

I can't believe that pussy ass nigga shot me; I can't beleive that pussy ass nigga shot me," he said. "Who shot you son," one of the gentlemen in the crowd of church people ask? "I don't know who shot me," he said.

He was lying like a motherfucker, who knew exactly who shot him.

"They called the police already, they should be here soon, it's a police station nearby," the gentlemen said.

In no time flat the police arrived first, and the ambulance arrived shortly after.

The guy that had got shot told the police he didn't know who shot him, although he did. He didn't want the nigga that shot him to get locked up, he wanted to kill the bitch.....

Several days later the guy was let out of the hospital but had to be in a wheel-chair, not for a long-term, only to his ass, and legs were well.....

The same day he was let out of the hospital, the same night the guy that shot him was killed, somebody shot him with a double barrel shotgun taking half his face off.

As homicide started their investigation they called it the face off murder. They never found any witnesses or suspects, so no one was never convicted or even charged with that murder.....

It seemed as if day by day the city streets, begin to be filled with madness, killings, mournings, sirens, and sadness.

It was clicks within the same gangs waring against each other. Rivals was waring against each other even harder. You had certain gangs that was into it with two different gangs at once. Then it was certain gangs that was into it with their own gang and into it with the opps all at the same time.

Part of the reason why gangs was tearing it up with each other was because years prior, and even to the present date the feds was locking up all the heads of gangs; everytime a new head would step up and get in play the Feds would find a way to lock his ass up to, leaving no law and order within the streets amongst; just like a body once you cut the heads off the body will fall. It was uncontrollable anarchy within the city streets.

Throughout the city streets it was constant gun-fire, like it was New Years Eve.

Some of the rappers changed the nickname from The Windy City to The City of No Pity.

Shit got so fucked up they start killing niggas in broad daylight on purpose.....

On one side of town two gangs was waring so hard they just start shooting at any and everybody that was affiliated with the oppositions.

One time they caught one of the opps main-girl walking the dog; they shot her and the dog. She lived the dog died.

The same nigga that girl and dog they shot, in return he caught an opp grandma-ma walking home from church with her bible in hand. He walked up to her upped a black .44 automatic to her stomach. Her smile instantly turned into a frown as she said, "praise the lord son," whole heartidely.

As he walked in the alley by gun point she didn't say a word, she wasn't scared at all not one bit, she feared no man but God.

As he walked her to the middle of the alley he seen a car slow down by the alley, he thought it was a detective car; he made her get on her knees on the side of a garbage can, he stood on the side of the garbage can faking like he was pissing. He immediately notice that it wasn't the police.

He looked down at her, she was on her knees praying. She wasn't worried about herself, she was praying for him, praying to the Heavenly Father that he would forgive him for his sins, and that someday he'd convert his life over to the Lord.....

Three shots ripped through her head, leaving her for dead, more blood to shed.

After the third shot many people came out on their back porches, not witnessing the actual murder, but witnessing seeing him fleeing from the scene of the crime.....

What the killer didn't know was that she was more than happy to die or be killed, because she knew that upon death she'd finally meet the king of kings, the lord of lords, God, and his only begotten son Jesus Christ to have eternal peaceful life in Heavens paradise.....

The same day the opps found out who killed his grandmother, him and his guys tore the streets up. The niggas from the other side tore it up as well they went round for round.

It was like a riot in the hoods they were from. They burned down houses, and cars, niggas from each side got shot up bad or killed.

They even burn up some houses waited until the opps came running out and shot them up murdered they ass.....

A few days after grandma was murdered homicide apprehendid the killer taking him to jail charging him with that murder. What the killer didn't know was that is that many people witness/saw him running up the alley after he shot her, and that he'd never see the streets again, he'd spend the rest of his natural life rotting away in a jail cell.....

All the violence brought forth more police harrasement of blacks.....

More protesting about Black Lives Matter.

In various places on each side of town you'd see large numbers of people on corners,

holding up signs saying honk your horn if you love Jesus, some of the people had on Black Lives Matter T-Shirts, as others had on All Lives Matter T-Shirts. Almost every car that road pass honked their horn, some hollered out "we love you Jesus, Black Lives Matter." A small percentage of passing cars parked their cars joining in on the peaceful protest.....

Upcoming Urban Fiction Novels by Alan Hines:

Scandalous Scandal

CHAPTER 1

A s Prince's song Scandalous slightly echoed in the room at a low pleasant tone through the surround sound speakers, as he constantly inhaled and exhaled the blunt filled with loud, relaxing he could visualize good things to be, making more money, and growth and development in the drug game.

And then he heard a knock on the door.....

Fontane opened the door and there she stood there with a brown trench coat on. Such a radiant beauty looking like a Goddess on Earth.....

Before she could step all the way in the door, in her own silent mind she admired the aroma of the wonderful smell of the loud smoke, as it made her slightly begin to cough.....

"Step in, I wasn't expecting you for another hour or two,"Fontane said. "My kids went to sleep early so I decided to come over while they was asleep. You promise you aren't going to tell anybody," she said. "Girl stop playing you know I aint gone tell nobody,"Fontane said. "I'm not like these other ho's that's always out here selling pussy, I'm just doing this because my man locked up, and I got bills to pay," she said.....

Without saying another word she stood up off the couch dropped the trench coat, and there she stood as naked as the day she was born. The biggest roundest prettiest titties imaginable she possessed. The pussy was so hairy looked like chinchilla fur. She turned around to show off her big ole ass.

His mouth dropped, and dick got so hard it felt like it was going to bust. He immediately took his clothes off. He wondered if he'd use a rubber or not, within seconds he made up his mind not to, he figured that if he was finna pay for the pussy he might as well get his money worth.....

As both of them was still standing he bent her over as she used her hands on the couch for stability, he forced his dick in her tight wet pussy, and begin fucking the shit out of her as if he was mad at the world.....Within five pumps he nutted unloaded all of it in her guts. She was disappointed, and pleased at the same time that he nutted so fast; she was disappointed because it felt so wonderful and she wanted the pleasure to be endless, but on the flip side she was pleased because she knew her pussy was a bomb in which made him nut quick.....

"Bend down and suck this dick bitch," Fontane said. "Boy watch your mouth," she said in a low soft tone.....

With no hesitation she got on her knees with an aim to please, to him her mouth was fantastic; she'd suck on the dick thoroughly, while strocking it with her right hand all at the same damn time.

In no time flat he was busting nuts down her throat; he couldn't believe it because it was hard for any chick to make him nut by sucking his dick.

He laid her on her back on the couch and begin squeezing and sucking her titties, as if he was breast feeding as she held her own legs up he begin giving her the dick in it's most harsh form as she continously begged for him to do it harder.....

For hours on and off they performed hardcore sex.....

As it was time to go she put on her high heels and trench coat as he stared, and watched admiring the view.....

"Okay nigga what's the hold up give me my four hundred," she said. "Here, here go six hundred whenever you need some financial assistance please let me know," Fontane said.

She snatched the money out his hand happy as a kid at Christmas time, as she waved at him, and told him bye.....

CHAPTER 2

Fontane begin to feel his phone vibrating. "Hello," Fontane said. "Hello can I speak to to Fontane," Chresha said. "Yeah this me, who is this," Fontane asked? "This is Chresha." "Why do everytime you call me you always ask to speak to me, and you know you calling my phone, I mean do that make any sense to you," Fontane asked? "Because I know sometimes you be having other people answer your phone," Chresha said. "Girl you know aint nobody answering my phone," Fontane said. "Why do you always ask who this is calling you, what you got another girlfriend or something," Chresha said. "You know damn well I'm not fucking with nobody but you," Fontane said. "Good game, real phony," she said.....

"I've been missing you and shit lately, you must got another bitch because you don't spend no time with me," Chresha said. "You know me I've been traveling state to state

doing business ventures," Fontane said. "Business ventures my ass, you been traveling state to state to buy dope," Chresha said. "Is you done lost your motherfucking mind, you can't be saying shit like that over the phone, the feds could have my phone tapped," Fontane said. "Nigga you aint on shit, the feds aint thinking about you, you aint moving enough product," Chresha said.....

Little did she know he was moving more than enough product for the Feds to be watching. His connect in Chicago was supplying him with enough dope to supply a third of Flint city.....

"I'm serious Chresha you gotta be careful of what you say over the phone cuz the Feds can popp a nigga ass for little petty shit they say over the phone. They'll have my ass way in the basement in the Feds joint across country, some motherfucking where," Fontane said.

"Well since you say I haven't been spending that much time with you, why don't you come over now, and wear one of them new lingerie sets under your clothes," Fontane said. "Which one you want me to wear," Chresha asked? "It don't matter just pick one of the newest ones," Fontane said. "A'ight I got you, I'm going to bring my sister with me," Chresha said. "For what," he asked with authority.....He hated her twin sister Teressa with a passion.

"I want to bring her over to do what you've been asking me to do," Chresha said. "What's that," he asked? "You know what you've been wanting me to do," Chresha said.

"What's that," Fontane asked again? "The threesome," she respond.....

His mouth dropped as he dropped the phone on the floor.....

He picked up the phone and immediately asked, "are you serious." "Yeah I'm serious we wanna do it," Chresha said.

"You trying to tell me that as much as me and your sister can't stand each other she wants me to fuck her," he said. "Yes, that's exactly what I'm saying," she said.....

Fontane paused for a minute in disbelief, and overjoyed that he was going to have a threesome with two twin sisters.

"A'ight, ya'll come on over here and bring some drinks with ya'll," Fontane said.

He went into the room popped a Viagara he stole from his grandfather, and an x-pill,

and then fired up a leaf joint. He rushed smoking his leaf joint; he was a closet leaf smoker he didn't want nobody to know he smoked leaf.....

Fontane sat back high as kite visualizing how beautiful the girls look; The twins looked just alike, short, thick ass hell, caramel complexion, smooth skin, dark brown eyes.....

In no time flat the girls were at his house; it seemed like they flew a private jet over there, because they came so fast.

The door bell ring twice; Fontane went to the door looked out his peep hole and to his surprise the girls were standing there. Like damn how they get over here that quick, he thought to himself.

He immediately opened the door before he could say a word Chresha put her index finger to her lips to sush him.

As Chresha and Teressa entered his home, Chresha locked the door. Both women grabbed him by each one of his hands and led him into his bedroom.

Inside Fontane felt like a kid again on the verge of it being his first time getting some pussy.

Within seconds both girls were in their birthday suits standing side by side each other, awaiting for him to undress and give out orders.

Fontane undressed and got on his knees on the bed; he ordered Chresha to suck his dick. Chresha got on the bed on all fours and begin sucking the shit out of his dick.

Teressa begin finger fucking Chresha ass and pussy with two fingers in each hole, right hand fingers in the pussy hole, left hand fingers in the asshole. Fontane couldn't believe what was taking place.

As Fontane was on the verge of busting a nut Teressa begin eating Chresha's pussy in which made his nut burst out like an erupting Volcano.

Fontane begin thinking to himself, these ho's done did this shit before; why they didn't been do this with me. These ho's some freaks doing insence, and everything.

Once Teressa completed eating Chresha out momentarily, Fontane told her to lay on the bed. She laid on the bed flat on her stomach as Fontane begin stuffing his dick in and out her pussy. Teressa laid on the bed watching them while sucking on the two fingers that she'd stuck in Chresha's ass while finger fucking herself with two fingers from her other hand.

Just when Fontane was getting ready to nut he told Teressa, "take your fingers outta your mouth and give me a kiss."

while Fontane and Teressa tongues intertwine she continued fingering herself as Fontane commence to stuff his dick into Chresha pussy.

Fontane then told Teressa to lay flat on her stomach as he begin to enter Teressa he could feel a big difference from Chresha; Teressa's pussy was much tighter, and moist. Now was his chance to take out all his anger, frustration, and dislike for Teressa out on her pussy.

He shoved his dick in her with force, and commenced to fucking her like he was mad at the world. She pleaded for him to stop as he continued going, giving her the dick in it's rawest form.

Once he unloaded his sperm cells in her she jumped up yelling, "I told you to stop." He grabbed her head and begin tongue kissing her, the kiss kinda put her at ease.

After he finished kissing Teressa he started kissing Chresha. Then Chresha and Teressa begin kissing one another.....

As Fontane maintained his composure, deep down within he was going wild inside.....

For hours into the morning came around without to many intermissions they fucked and

sucked one another.....

As the night turned into morning all three sat and watched the sun rise will listening to Jazz at a low tone. They laughed and talked reminiscing about last night making plans to do it again.

They ended up showering seperately as everybody went their seperate ways; but right before they left the house Fontane told them, "I'm a call ya'll later on." "Make sure you do," Chresha said.

He hugged both girls and they left, and went their seperate ways.

Fontane fired up a Newport Long and got on the phone to call his guy Rob.....

"Rob guess who I fucked last night," Fontane said. "Who is this," Rob asked? "This Fontane, guess who I fucked last night," Fontane said. "Who," Rob asked? "I fucked Chresha and Teressa together," Fontane said. "No you didn't, get your ass outta here," Rob said. "On my momma I fucked Chresha, and Teressa, and they fucked each other," Fontane said. "Straight up, did they," Rob said. "Yup," Fontane said. "How you pull that off you must of paid for that," Rob said? "Naw I didn't pay, shiit I would've thou," Fontane said, as they both begin laughing.....

"I've been sweating Chresha to have a threesome with me and another woman for a long ass time. So yesterday she call me on some emotional shit talking about we aint been spending very much time together, and some other ole goofy ass shit she was talking about. So I told her to come on over to my crib. She tells me that her and Teressa wanted to do a threesome. At first I thought she was bullshitting because Teressa and me can't stand each other. Come to find out she wasn't bullshitting. They came straight over and got to work. Them ho's done did that shit before," Fontane said. "When you gonna set them out to the guys," Rob asked? "Not yet later," Fontane said. "Why not know instead of later," Rob asked? "I already know how they is it's gonna take a while for them to do it with somebody else," Fontane said.....

Fontane was lying he didn't wanna set them out, he loved Chresha.

"A man I gotta go to the cleaner's, I'll catch up with you later on," Fontane said. "A'ight man I holler at you, love nigga," Rob said. "Love," Fontane said.

Later on that night Fontane cell phone rang.....

"Hello," Fontane said. "I thought you said you was gonna call us," Chresha said. "I got caught in some business deals, other than that I would've call," Fontane said. "Come over here tonight me and Teressa wanna see you, and spend some time with you," Chresha said. "I can't I'm in the middle of some business right now, other than that I'll be there; I promise I'll be over there tomorrow for sho," Fontane said. "I gotta work tomorrow," Chresha said. "Well I'll come over there after work, but before I hang up what made you, and

Teressa wanna do that with me," Fontane asked? "I love you, and shit and I'll do anything for you," Teressa said.....

Fontane remained quiet for a seconds pleased with her answer made him feel like a player.....

"But what made Teressa wanna do that," Fontane asked? "She really like you," Chresha said. "Now you know damn well me and Teressa can't stand each other," Fontane said. "That's what you thought, she always liked you," Chresha said. "Be for real, Teressa is the only person I ever met that I argue with everytime we're around," Fontane said. "You just didn't know deep down inside, she liked you, and always wanted to give you some of that pussy," Chresha said.....

Fontane paused for the matter of seconds letting it mirinate in his head.....oh well fuck it if they wanna have threesomes who gives a fuck if she likes me or not, Fontane thought to himself.....

"But uhhh anyway tell Teressa I said, what's up," Fontane said. "A'ight," Chresha said. "I gotta go," Fontane said. "Promise you'll be over here tomorrow when I get off work," Chresha said. "I promise," Fontane said. "I love you," Chresha said. "A'ight I'll holla," Fontane said as the both ended their call.....

The next day Fontane came over and picked up Teressa while Chresha was at work. He took her shopping spent five hundred on 2 pair of high heel shoes.....

Afterwards they went to the show. Once the movie was over they road around town ended up naked, sexing at a sleazy motel.....

Teressa, and Chresha lived together. Once he took Teressa home he had a long talk with her. "Teressa now you know what goes on between me and you stays between me and you," Fontane said. "What do you mean by that," Teressa asked? "Whatever we do when Chresha aint around is between you, and I," Fontane said. "You know damn well I aint no dummy, I aint gonna tell Chresha that we fucked and you took me shopping when she wasn't around, let me tell you a little secret," Teressa said. "What's that," Fontane asked? "I always liked your stanking ass," Teressa said. "You showl gotta a way with showing people you like them," Fontane said. "That's just the way I am, I'm snotty as hell; well anyway let's not bring up old shit," Teressa said.....

She begin to smile genuinely as if she was happy than she ever been in life.....

"You know me and my sister will do anything for you. Whatever we can do to make you happy we're all for it, seeing you happy will only make us more happier," Teressa said.....

He slowly moved his face towards hers as their tongues collided, as he was trying to kiss her, and suck her lips and tongue all at once.

He then stood her up pulled her pants down to her knees. Then pulled his pants down to his knees, bent her over and gave her the dick hardcore in the rawest form.....

Afterwards they sat down and watched some midget porn until they dosed off and went to sleep.....

By the time Chresha came in from work Teressa, and Fontane were fully dressed sound asleep on the couch.....

Chresha walked through the door seen him on the couch and instantly began smiling.....

Chresha walked slowly over to him, dropped her purse took off all her clothes, and laid them on the floor.

She tapped him gently on his head..... "Wake up sleepy head," Chresha said.

He opened his eyes as his vision was a little blurry.

Once his sight became clearer he came to focus on Chresha standing up ass hole naked.

She put her index finger on her lips to ssssh him. Grabbed his hand and led him into the bedroom. She gently closed the door and locked it, got on her knees unbutton, and unzipped his pants grabbed his dick firmly and commenced in attempts to suck the skin off it.

In the process of sucking his dick she could taste and smell pussy; right than and there she knew him and Teressa was fucking while she was at work. she had no problem with it nor was she going to comfront him about it, she figured fuck it let him have his fun.

As he begin squirting his nut down her throat she swallowed it all.....

"Stand up and bend over," Fontane said.....

He pulled his pants to his knees and begin giving her every inch of his dick as she turned her face towards him as is she was looking at him, but in reality she wasn't her eyes was closed. He enjoyed the pleasure of the sight of her ass jiggling, and seeing her fuck faces.

As he begin to nut it felt like the best nut he'd ever released in life, it felt good.

After sexing Chresha went and showered and dressed and woke Teressa up as the three of them went on there expedition of a day, and night filled with excitement.

They kicked it like they were celebrating some sort of victory.....

They started of by simply riding down town area popping bottles as Chresha and Teressa flashed their breast to pedestrians.

They ended up at a dance club.

As they walked in the dance club it was as if they were the center of attraction,

as Jay Rule remake of Stevie Wonder's song Giving It Up echoed in the speakers they begin dancing on the dance floor as if they owned it.

They got so drunk at the club that Teressa forgot were she was at.

Bottles after bottles, going back and forth to the dance floor, and to the photographer taking pictures all night.

They even found a way to take a few puffs of a little weed in the midst of the of all the cigarette smoke, without security catching them.

That night seemed as if all them became closer to one another.....

On their way home from the club they listened to continious 2Pac CD's in a mildly tone while reminiscing about all the fun times they had over time with, and without each other.

Once they made it to Chresha, and Teressa house Teressa and Fontane went straight to sleep, because they was so intoxicated.

Chresha undressed Fontane and Teressa. She took turns sucking on Fontane's dick, and eating Teressa's pussy until she got tired and went to sleep herself.....

After that night Fontane and the girls became real close.

Fontane even stop hanging out with the guys alot because he begin to fall in love with the girls, they had him sprung.

They girls even begin to help Fontane conduct his drug business.

CHAPTER 3

Fontane's connect in Chicago started flooding him with more, and more cocaine; the happiness of love through financial gain came to life, became.

Fontane's connect would supply him with some of the purest cocaine around town.

Each day Fontane started to make more and more money than he'd normally make.

Fontane didn't sell no petty nickels and dimes he sold straight weight.

The more money he made the more money the girls were able to enjoy of his.

The twins would go shopping when ever they got ready. They both had numerous cars eqipped with rims, sounds, and Lamborghini doors.

Fontane really loved the girls and would do anything for them.

The twins on the other hand didn't give a fuck about him, they never did.

The only thing they cared about was more dollar signs.

These ho's stop working they had it made.

That was the only reason they started fucking with him in the beginning was to trick him outta all his doe.

They plan was to both begin sexing him, get him to trust them, and trick him into falling in love to benefit off his wealth, and their plan worked.

These ho's had more game than Milton Bradley. They was thorough in the way they schemed for money.

Only eighteen but had more game then the average women twice their age.

Their game came from all the things they heard and seen. They had enough game to turn filthy animals clean. They could talk preachers into being sinners, turn losers to winners.

Their mom and dad was drug addicts, the rest of their small family was caught up living their own lives, and really didn't give a fuck about the twins. So at an early age the twins had to scheme for money to survive, and they did it well.

It's a sad repition cycle of broken homes, shattered black family structure contrary to the past times of our lives, of days, lives of yesterday, when blacks lived in two parent homes, only addictions was worshipping God within a sense pleasurable tone.....

Throughout sex they'd take him places he never been before. Not just physically but mentally as well. Those ho's had mastered the art of seduction.

These ho's was something else.

Although these ho's was only eighteen they looked every bit of twenty five.

They looked like super models. You'd see them and couldn't tell they was ghetto at all.

They was beautiful, lovely and free as artwork of paintings from God to be mutual.

Many men would stop and stare imagining if they could have atleast one to love frequently suitable.

The twins stood 5.5 and gorgeous enough to give sight to the blind. Smooth caramel skin with caramel brown eyes to match. They wore no make up because they was naturally beautiful.

The twins were identical, other difference was they wore different hair styles. They always kept their hair down, lips juiced up, and nails, and toes done.

The twins made Fontane feel supreme like a emperor or a king; on top of the world above the clouds as it seems, fairy tale turned to reality formulated from a sweet dream.....

CHAPTER 4

More and more for Fontane clientale blossomed grew. More money that was being made Fontane was enjoying life as far as going out clubbing and having fun.

One night Fontane was already high as the clouds that descend in the sky on this place formally known as Earth, he decided to go to a club in which his homie Snake invited him to earlier the same week.

Once he made in the club as if he was stuck in his pleasure mode of time, although their were many others of course in the club it seems as if Fontane was in a world of his own.....

It took him a little while to find Snake but once he did it brought joy to Snake seeing Fontane there as they begin smiling at one another.....

Fontane stepped to Snake, Snake hugged Fontane firmly as if he hadn't seen him within the ages of time.

Snake spoke in Fontane's ear, "it's good to see you", Fontane spoke in Snake's ear, "it's good to see you to". They both had to shout loud because the music was at an all time high.

Snake popped open a bottle of Champagne as it splashed all over Fontane's shirt. Snake tried to apologize but Fontane didn't give a fuck.

"Damn nigga I want Champagne in my glass, not on my shirt," Fontane said as they begin laughing. "Nigga you look like you already wasted." Snake said.

Snake drunk Champagne straight out the bottle, passed it to Fontane as he drunk straight out the bottle as well.

Fontane and Snake went to the dance floor and danced with damn near half the chicks on the dance floor, showing out acting a fool with it.

Within a couple of hours Fontane was to drunk to continue partying.....

"Hey man I'm finna call it a night man, I'll get up with you tomorrow," Fonatne said. "The night just begun," Snake said. "Maybe for you, but I'm finna go home," Fontane said. "So which ho you gonna take home with you," Snake asked? "Nam one I'm finna go home and go to sleep," Fontane said. "Do you want me to drop you off at home," Snake asked? "Naw man I'm cool," Fontane said. "You sure man, you know it's plenty of family members here I can have one of them drop you off, Lord knows you don't need no D.U.I.'s, I'd hate for something to happen to you," Snake said. "Naw B I'm straight, trust me," Fontane said.

As Fontane left the club Snake stared at him, thinking to himself I shouldn't let this drunk ass nigga drive home by himself he might have an accident or something.

Once Fontane left the club Snake continued to party as if this was his last day on Earth.....

On the ride home Fontane felt himself getting ready to throw up; he instantly pulled over, opened the door as he remained seated he bent over and begin throwing up. Outta nowhere a gun man came and shot him three times in the back his head, and one in the neck.Took his life line from him never got a chance to see who done it.....

As the cops arrived, yellow tape to the perimeter; they begun their investigation only witness was homeless man he said the only thing he knew was that he heard gun shots, and seen firely sparks from a gun but didn't see who done it. The police continued to question the homeless man asking him how could he see firely sparks come from a gun but didn't see who did the killing; the homeless man continue to contend that he didn't see who did the killing which was the truth.....

Years later homicide never ever found the killer. Fontane's own guys couldn't find the killer didn't even know who did it and why.....

A week after Fontane was killed his funeral was held the twins sat in the front row crying Crocodile tears; in reality they wasn't crying because Fontane was dead they was crying because Fontane was their financial support.

Snake sat in the back of the church feeling guilty remaining silent, in his own silent mind it felt it was his fault. I knew I should'nt have let Fontane go home by himself, Snake thought to himself.

As the line proceeded to view Fontane's dead body Fontane's momma went to the casket and begin fixing Fontane's suit collar, and begin hollering in Fontane's face. "Why him, why, why, why, him. Why ya'll have to take my son. I hope whomever did this shit die a thousands deaths," she said as tears dripped down her face like the flowing of pouring rain and pain.

One of Fontane's homies grabbed Fontane's mom hugged her and told her Fontane is going to a better place.

"Bitch take your nasty ass hands off me," Fontane's mom said as she slapped him and spit in his face.

"It's cause of you bitches my son is died. If he wouldn't been fucking around the B.D.'s my son would still be living.....

She ran to the middle of the church took off all her clothes upped a box cuter, and said I hope all you bitches die me and my son we lived in this world together, and we shall die together; right then and there she slide her own throat hideously taking her own life away. As suicide is an unforgiving sin she'll never reach the pearly gates within the sky. The box cuter fell to the ground as blood ran from her neck she stumbled momentarily than fell to the ground as the crowds came to her rescue.

They rushed her to the hospital she was pronounced dead on arrival.

After they found she was dead they went back to Fontane's funeral and took his body to be buried.....

A week later Fontane's mom funeral was held at the same church. They buried Fontane's mom right next to Fontane.

Family members and friends never stop grieving over the loss of Fontane and his mom; it was like a mental torture chamber of pain.....

Chapter samples of previously published
Urban Fiction Novels by Alan Hines:

Queen of Queens

PROLOGUE

It was the summer of July 4th 1971, 11:30 P.M.,in Chicago as the fireworks lit up the skies.

CHAPTER 1

"You sure this the right spot man"Slim asked? "I'm positive this is the right spot,I wouldn't never bring you on no blank mission,"Double J said.

With no hesitation Double J kicked in the door and yelled,"Police lay the fuck down".

Double J and Slim stormed in the crib with guns in hand ready to fuck a nigga up if anybody made any false moves.

As they entered the crib they immediately noticed two women sitting at the table;the women was getting ready to shake up some dope.

One of the women laid on the floor face down,crying out"please,please don't shoot me".....

She had seen many t.v. shows and movies in which the police kicked in doors and wrongfully thought an individual was strap or reaching for a gun when they wasn't,as the police hideously shot them taking their life line from em.

The other woman tried to run and jump outta the window; before she could do so Double J tackled her down and handcuffed her.

Double J threw Slim a pair of handcuffs,"handcuff her",Double J said.As Slim begin to handcuff the other chick he begin thinking to himself,were the fuck this nigga get some motherfucking handcuffs from.

The woman that was on the floor crying looked up and noticed that Slim wasn't the police.

"You niggas ain't no motherfucking police,"she said. Double J ran over and kicked her in the face,and busted her nose.

"Bitch shut the fuck up",Double J said.She shut up,laid her head on the floor.As her head was filled with pain,while tears ran down her face,with blood running from her nose she silently prayed that this real life nightmare would come to an end!

Simultaneously Slim and Double J looked at the table filled with dope. Both Slim and Double J mouths drop;they'd never seen so much dope in their lives. Right in front of their eyes was 100 grams of pure uncut heroin.

Both women laid on the floor scared to death;they'd never been so scared in their natural lives.

Double J went into the kitchen found some zip lock bags,came back and put the dope in them,and then stuffed the dope in the sleeves of his jacket cause it was too much dope to fit in his pockets.

"Man we gotta hurry up,you know the neighbors probably heard us kick the door in,"Slim said."The neighbors ain't heard shit cuz of all the fireworks going off.That's why I picked this time to run off in here,while the fireworks going off so nobody won't hear us,"Double J said. "Shiit they could've still heard us,the fireworks ain't going off inside the building,"Slim said."Don't worry about it,"Double J said.

"Lord lets search the rooms before we leave,you know if all this dope is here it gotta be some guns or money in here somewhere,"Double J said."Yep,Jo I bet you it is,"Slim said.

Double J walked over to the woman whom nose he busted kneeled to his knees put a .357 to her ear and clicked the hammer back.

The woman heard the hammer click in her ear,she became so scared that she literally shitted on herself.

"Bitch am a ask you one time,where the rest of that shit at,"Double J asked in a deep hideous voice? She begin crying out and yelling,"it's in the closet in the bottom of the dirty cloths hamper."

Double J went into the closet snatched all the cloths outta the hamper and found ten big bundles of money. He seen a book bag hanging in the closet,grabbed it and loaded the money in it.

Double J went back into the front room, without second guessing it he shot both women in the back of their heads two times a piece.

Double J and Slim fled from the apartment building,got into their steamer and smashed off.

As Double J drove a few blocks away Slim sat in the passenger side of the car looking over at Double J pissed off.

"Lord,why the fuck you shoot them ho's,"Slim asked with hostility? "Look at all the money and dope we got,"Double J said."What that gotta do with it,"Slim asked? "You know that,that wasn't them ho's shit,they was working for some nigga,and if that nigga ever found out we stuck him up for all that shit he'd have a price on our heads.Now that the only people who knew about us taking that shit is dead we don't gotta worry about that shit,"Double J said. Yeah you right about that,Slim thought to himself as he remained silent for a few seconds.....

"You just said something about dope and money,what money,"Slim asked? "Look in the book bag,"Double J said.

Slim unzipped the book bag and it was as he'd seen a million dollars.His mouth dropped,amazed by all the money that was in the book bag.

They hit the e-way and set fire to a lace joint as they begun to think of all of the things they'd be able to do with the money and dope.....

Double J and Slim were two petty hustlers looking for this one big lick,and they finally got it.

They had various hustles that consist of robbing,car theiving,and selling a little dope. All their hustles revovled around King Phill. King Phill was a king of a branch of ViceLords,the(I.V.L.) Insane Vice Lords. They'd rob,steal cars,and sell dope through King Phill,one way or the other.

Double J and Slim were basically King Phill's yes men. Whatever Phill would say or wanted them to do they'd say yes to.

After 45 minutes of driving they parked the steamer on a deserted block where there was no houses,only a big empty park.

Double J begin wiping off the inside of the car.Slim begin to do the same.

"Make sure you wipe off everything real good,we don't wanna leave no fingerprints,"Double J said."You aint gotta tell me, that's the last thing I wanna do is get pinched for a pussy ass stick up murder,"Slim said.

Double J put the book bag on his back and they left the car wiping off the inside and outside door handles and they begin walking to Double J's crib,which was about thirty minutes away.

"Lord fire up one of them lace joints,"Slim said."Here you fire it up,"Double J said as he passed the joint to Slim. Slim instantly set fire to it.They walked swiftly to Double J's crib,continuously puffing on the lace joints.

Once they made it halfway there,out of nowhere,Double J stopped in his tracks.

"What the fuck you stop for,"Slim asked? "Lord we gotta get rid of that car,"Double J said."Why,"Slim asked? "Cuz,like you said we don't wanna get pinched for no stick up murder.If somebody seen that car leave the scene of the crime and they tell the police and the police find the car and dust it for fingerprints,and find one fingerprint that matches one of ours we booked. We'll be sitting on death row saying what we should've,would've,and could've done,"Double J said."How we gone get rid of it,"Slim asked?

"Here take my gun and bookbag,and meet me at my crib,my girl there she'll let you in,"Double J said.

"You still didn't answer my question,"Slim said. "What's that,"Double J asked? "How we gone get rid of the car,"Slim asked? "Don't worry about it,I got it,"Double J said. "Let's get rid of it together,"Slim said. "Naw man we need to make sure the money and dope is safe,and we need to get these hot ass guns off the streets,"Double J said. "Where is the dope,"Slim asked?

Double J reached in his sleeves pulled out the dope and handed it all to Slim as they departed and went their separate ways.....

I hope this nigga don't get caught fucking around with that car, Slim thought to himself.

Double J went back to the car looking for something to use to set it on fire with.

He ended up finding some charcoal fluid in the trunk of the car, squeezed all the fluid out of the bottle all over the car, struck a match and threw it on the car as it instantly begin burning.

Double J took off running.He ran halfway home,and walked the other half.

Once Double J made it home,before he could even knock on the door or ring the doorbell Slim opened the door. Double J rushed in nervously and slammed the door behind himself and frantically locked it.

"Nigga what the fuck took you so long,"Slim asked? "What took me so long,shiiit I ran halfway back,but anyway I took care of the business,I burned the car up,"Double J said.

"How much dough we got,"Double J asked? "I don't know I ain't even open the book bag up,I was waiting to you get here,"Slim said. "See thats why I fuck with you,anybody else would've played me for some of the money and dope,"Double J said. "You my nigga I would'nt never try to get over on you.To keep it real, you didn't even have to take me on the lick with you,"Slim said.....

They went into the bathroom,locked the door and begin counting the money.Each bundle of money was a G.

"Damn lord we got 10 stacks and all this dope,"Slim said.

"How we gone get rid of all this dope,"Double J asked? "We gone sell it in grams,"Slim said. "Naw man we need to sell it in bags,we'll make more money selling it in bags.The only problem is where we gone sell it at,you know anywhere we try to open up at they gone close us down,"Double J said. "We gone sell it in the hood,"Slim said. "Stop playing you know damn well we dead in the hood. You know if we open up in the hood they gone close us straight down,"Double J Said. "We gone have to go through Phill,"Slim said. "Yeah we'll get up with Phill tomorrow,"Double J said.

"Man don't tell nobody where we got the dope from,"Double J said. "Nigga,do I look like a lame to you? What the fuck I look like telling somebody about what we did,"Slim said.

"I'm finna go to sleep,you might as well spend a night,"Double J said. "Yeah I might as well spend a night,"Slim said."I'll holla at you in the morning,I'm sleepy as hell,"Double J said as he started to yawn. As Slim went and laid on the couch in the living room. Double J went into his bedroom undressed down to his boxers and t-shirt and got into bed with his wife who he assumed was asleep.

As Double J pulled the covers back he noticed that his wife was in bed asshole naked.

I'm glad I married her,Double J thought to himself while enjoying the view.....

Slim and Double J stayed awoke for a little while thinking about the money they had and the profit they was going to make off the dope.....

As Double J closed his eyes to go to sleep he felt his wife's hands gently slipping into his boxers rubbing on his dick.

"I thought you were asleep,"Double J said."I ain't sleep,I was just laying here thinking about you,"she said.

She continued rubbing on his dick.

"Now you know you can't be rubbing on my dick without any lubrication.That shit don't feel good when you do it with dry hands,"Double J said.

She got up and squeezed a little Jergens in the palm of her hand,as he slipped his boxers off and laid back on the bed.

She grabbed his dick firmly,begin lathering it up with the lotion and jagging him off at the same time.

As she thoroughly jagged him off he pumped her hand until his nut unleashed on her titties,as she begin rubbing the nut around on her titties as if it was baby oil or lotion.

She then took his dick into her mouth gobbling it and the lotion in all swirling her tongue around it and sucking on it as if she was trying to suck some sweet nectar out of it.

Once it got rock hard she begin deep throating it,choking herself with his dick while rubbing on her own clitoris roughly while humming.

In no time flat he was releasing a load of nut down her throat.

She stood up,wiped her mouth and slightly begin growling she then got on top of him and played with his dick for a few seconds until it got back hard.

She looked him in his eyes,as she grabbed his dick firmly and shoved it in her pussy,and begin smiling.....

She begin riding it slowly to get her pussy totally wet,as he grabbed her ass cheeks guiding her movements.

Once her pussy got wet he begin slamming his dick in and out of her,enjoying the tightness of her moist pussy.As she clawed his chest moaning in the midst of pleasure and pain;she liked when it hurted.

It felt so good to him that every time he'd slam his dick up in her pussy it felt like he was actually nutting each time.

As Double J begin to nut,she was cumming simultaneously as he begin to slam his dick in and out her pussy rougher and harder,she begin fucking him back;it was like a rodeo show as their orgasms exploded.

"Get up,get on the bed so I can hit it from the back,"Double J said.She got on all fours on the bed.

Double J got on his knees right behind her and began squeezing and rubbing her big brown pretty ass cheeks.

"Tell me you love me before you start fucking me,"she said."I love your hot ass,"he said.

Double J then rammed his dick in her hot pussy gripping her ass cheeks and slamming his dick in and out her pussy hard and fast while admiring the way her ass cheeks bounced.

In no time he was letting another nut explode in her pussy.

"Let me suck it,"she said in a low seductive tone."Hold on let me roll up a joint,"Double J said."You know that I don't like the smell of lace joints,why you got to lace your weed with cocaine? Why you can't smoke regular weed like everybody else,"she said.

Double J begin smiling,and looking her straight in the eyes.

"We'll I'll smoke a regular joint just for you,"Double J said.

He rolled up a regular joint with only weed in it. Set fire to it as she got on her knees with an aim to please.

As he inhaled and exhaled the potent weed smoke she simultaneously sucked his dick utilizing a suction method sucking mainly the tip thoroughly.

From the potent effect of the weed,combined with her superb suction method, and the moisture of her mouth felt so good that within seconds he released a glob of nut in her face.

He finished smoking his joint and both of them laid on the bed.

"You must really been wanting to fuck?,"Double J asked. "I been thinking about you all day at work. I had to take off work because I creamed in my panties daydreaming about your dick going in and out my pussy and mouth. I been sitting in the house all day waiting on you,"she said.

I done married a freak,Double J thought to himself.

They begin to tell each other how much they loved one another.And how their lives wouldn't be the same without each other,before both of them fell

into a deep sleep.....

The next morning after Double J's wife had went to work Double J and Slim sat at the kitchen table eating breakfast,reminiscing about the stick up and the murders.

They glorified and celebrated the stick up and the murders as if they were professional athletes that just won a championship game,or as if they had won the lottery.

It's sad how bloodshed make others glad.But this life some live as thugs consist of no love.

Other people were brought up to increase the peace and strive to earn college degrees,and live the American dream.

But those that live the street life thrive on death and destruction;they rob,steal,and kill with no discretion,and glorify others name that do the same.....

"Hurry up and finish eating so we can go holla at Phill,"Double J said."I'm already finished,"Slim said. "Well empty the rest of that shit that's on the plate in the garbage and put that plate in the sink,"Double J said.

Slim emptied the rest of the food in the garbage and put the plate in the sink,and went and grabbed the book bag.

"Naw we gone leave the dope and shit here unless you wanna take your half to your house,"Double J said."It's cool,I'll leave it here,"Slim said.

As they rode up the block in the hood where Phill was they noticed many of the Insanes on Phill's security as usual.

Once they made it to where Phill was,Phill began smiling cuz he was happy to see them he needed them to take care of some business for him.

King Phill was a pretty boy.Stood about 6'5 half latino,half black with naturally curly black hair in his mid twenties.

For those that didn't know Phill personally that would've never believed that he was a king of a large street gang.King Phill looked like a pretty boy college student.....

"Park the car I need to holla at ya'll,"Phill said.

They parked and got out to holla at him.

"I need ya'll to get some steamers for me,"Phill said. "We ain't on no car thieving shit right now,we need your assistance on some other shit,"Double J said. "What ya'll need?"Phill asked.

"Let's step away from everybody it's personal,"Slim said.

As they stepped away from everybody else Phill begin trying to figure out what Double J,and Slim wanted. Maybe they finna ask for some shit Phill thought to himself.

"Phill we got some dope we need to get it off,"Double J said. "What you talking about,"Phill asked? "We need to pop it off in the hood,"Slim said. "What ya'll talking about opening up a dope spot in the hood,"Phill asked? "That's exactly what we're talking about,"Slim said. "You know ya'll can't work in the hood if ya'll ain't a 5 star universal elite,"Phill said. "I told him,"Double J said. "Well make us universal elites,"Slim said.

Phill begin laughing.....

"I don't just give out status like that, I ain't one of these phony ass nigga's that let people buy status, you gotta earn it fucking with me," Phill said.

Slim looked at Phill like he was crazy.....

"Earn it, all the shit we do for you, and for the hood. While them niggas you made universal elites be in the Bahamas some motherfucking where, we be doing all the shootings for the hood, and all type of other shit for you and the hood," Slim said. "Yeah you do got a point, cuz ya'll do stand on nation business. This what I'm going to do for ya'll. Am a let ya'll work in the hood under my name, but ya'll gotta pay," Phill said. "How much we gotta pay," Slim asked? "That depends on how much dope ya'll got," Phill said. "We got ten grams," Double J said..... He was lying. "Ten grams that ain't shit. Ya'll work them ten grams for two or three weeks outta Argale park. In two or three weeks ya'll should've atleast double or tripled them ten grams. Once ya'll do ya'll gotta give me a stack every week," Phill said.....

Double J and Slim looked at each other smiling knowing it was finna be on.

"A stack a week we got you," Double J said.

"We'll holla at you, I gotta go pick my girl up from work," Double J said..... He was lying.....

As Double J and Slim got into the car and rode off listening to Al Green's Love and Happiness they were happier than a kid on Christmas Day.....

CHAPTER 2

Three Days Later

"How much is that small black digital scale," Double J asked the cashier? "That one right there is a hundred dollars. But I'd recommend this white one right here if you're going to be weighing things over twenty eight grams. Alot of customers usually buy that small black one, then later on down the line the same customers come back and buy a bigger one, which is a waste of money to me," the woman cashier said. "How much do the white one cost," Slim asked? "Two hundred," the cashier said. "We'll take it," Slim said. "Will that be it," the cashier asked? "Naw we need five bottles of dorms, and a bundle of them little black baggies right there, and two of them mac spoons," Slim said.....

As other customers walked into small record store the cashier paused and begun covering up the small area where contraband was being sold.

"Thomas, can you service the new customers," the female cashier said to her co-worker.....

"Wait til these customers leave, then I'll give ya'll, ya'll items," the female cashier said to Double J and Slim.....

"Ya'll sell scales, baggies, and all type of shit to everybody in the city, and now you wanna act like it's top secret," Slim said. "Yeah we do supply alot of people with contraband, but those are only the people that come in here asking for it. We can't have contraband on display because it's all type of people that come in here. A person might come in here with their kids. Or an off duty police officer might come in here to buy some records. And if they see all of this contraband on display they'll report our ass to the city. We won't loose our store or anything like that, but we'll have to pay a healthy fine," the cashier said.....

Within minutes the other customers purchased their records and left the store.....

"Your total will come out to $375.00," she said.....

Slim paid her and they left the store.....

Once they made it to Double J's crib they immediately weighed the dope for the first time.....

"Damn lord we got a hundred grams, I thought it'll be about fifty grams," Slim said. "Yeah me to," Double J said. "Aw we finna put up numbers if this shit is a bomb," Slim said. "Showl is," Double J said.

"Why did you buy baggies instead of aluminum foil," Double J asked? "Cuz we gone put the dope in the baggies, we don't need no aluminum foil," Slim said. "But we need to put it in the aluminum foil so it can stay fresh," Double J said. "Once we put it in the baggies, then put some thick clear tape on the baggies the dope will stay fresh," Slim said.

"We need to find us a connect on some quinine," Double J said. "Naw we aint gone put no quinine or none of that other crazy shit on the dope. We either gone use dorms or sell it with no mix on it at all," Slim said.

"We gone put three pills on each gram of dope," Slim said.

"How many grams we gone bag up the first time," Double J asked? "We gone bag up ten grams first and put it out there and see what it do, you know we can't bag up to much cuz if it don't sell quick enough it'll fall off," Slim said. "That's my point exactly, that's why I ask," Double J said.

Double J weighed out ten grams on the scale. Then Double J and Slim opened up thirty dorms which was actually capsules. Double J and Slim then grabbed two playing cards a piece and begin mixing the dope with the dorms.....

"How many mac spoons we gone use," Double J asked? "We gone give up two macs for a sawbuck and see how that go first. I'f the dope is a bomb we gone drop down to one mac spoon or a mac and a half. That all depends on how good the dope is. And if it's real good we gone put more dorms on it," Slim said.

Double J and Slim grabbed a mac spoon a piece and begin measuring the dope, and putting it in the bags.....

"I got some thick clear tape in my room in the closet," Double J said. "Wait to we get finished before you go get it," Slim said.....

After about an hour and a half they'd finally finished bagging up the dope.....

"Let's count it up to see how much we bagged up," Double J said.

"We gone put twelve blows in a pack, whoever sell the pack get twenty dollars, and turn us in a hundred," Slim said. "How much we gone pay people to run the joint," Double J asked? "We ain't worried about that right now we gone run the joint ourselves. Once it pick up then we'll put people in play to run the joint. We'll worry about what we gone pay them when that time come," Slim said.....

As they sat at the table counting up the dope Slim begin to wonder who was they gone get to work the packs.....

"Shiiit who we gone get to work the joint," Slim asked? "My lil cousins gone work the joint. They been sweating me for the last couple days about when we gone open up the joint, so they can work. They juvenilles, so if they catch a case they momma's can just sign them out from the police station," Double J said.....

Once they finished counting the dope up it came out to twenty packs, and seven odds. They bagged up

$2,070 not including the two blows in each pack for the pack workers to get paid.....

Slim begin doing the mathematics in his head.....

"So if we got two stacks off ten grams then we gone get atleast twenty stacks off of the whole hundred grams," Slim said. "Shiit we gone get more than that if the dope is a bomb, and if it can take more than three pills a gram," Double J said. "Yep showl is," Slim said.

"Go grab the tape outta the closet," Slim said.....

When he came back with the tape Slim examined it.....

"Yeah joe this tape perfect," Slim said.....

They put twelve bags on a strip of tape, then put another strip of tape over the bags.

They put the tape over the bags in order for the dope to stay fresh, and so none of the workers wouldn't dip in the bags.....

Double J and Slim grabbed the dope and a .45 automatic and went to pick up Double J's cousins, and set up shop in Argale Park.....

They posted up and the corners and in the park.

One of Double J's cousin walked through the hood telling all the dope fiends that they were passing out free dope in Argale Park. They dopefiends rushed to the park and spreaded the word.....

The two niggas that stood in the park, Double J's cousin was the ones passing out the samples to the dopefiends.....

A couple hours later the park was filled with dopefiends shopping for dope.

Double J and Slim couldn't believe how fast, and how many dopefiends were coming to buy dope.

Judging by the large amount of dopefiends that were coming to buy dope, so soon, Double J and Slim knew they had some good dope.

"Damn lord look how many dopefiends waiting in line to shop," Slim said. "That's cuz the dopefiends that we gave samples to went and told everybody that we got good dope, word of mouth travel," Double J said.

Within two days and one night Double J and Slim sold the whole hundred grams.....

"Lord who we gone buy some more dope from," Slim asked? "That's a good question," Double J said.

As they continue to smoke and ride through the hood they remained silent trying to figure out who they'd start buying weight on the dope from.

"We gone have to start buying from Phill," Double J said. "Phill got good dope but it aint a bomb," Slim said. "How you know, you don't even use dope," Double J said. "I can tell from the numbers his dope spots put up. His spots put up a little numbers but they aint all that," Slim said. "Who else we gone buy dope from, we gone have to get it from Phill," Double J said.....

"Ride through Lexington and see if he out there," Slim said.....

As they made it on Lexington they seen Phill standing on the corner with a gang of niggas standing around him on his security.....

"A Phill check it out Lord," Slim said.....

Phill walked towards them smiling.....

"Where's my money at," Phill said. "What money," Slim asked? "My g, what else money. I heard ya'll been tipping outta the park," Phill said. "We'll get the money we owe you a little later on," Slim said. "It aint even been a whole week," Double J said. "So what I want my money, ya'll been tipping," Phill said. "Aigh't we got you," Double J said.

"How much you'll sell us twenty five grams of dope for," Slim asked? "Three thousand," Phill said. "That's kinda high aint it," Double J said. "Naw that's low, anybody else I charge one fifty a gram. I'm only charging ya'll like one twenty five a gram, at one twenty five a gram twenty five grams suppose to come out to thirty one twenty five, but I just said a even three stacks, I aint tripping over a hundred and twenty five dollars. Look right I got shit I gotta do, is ya'll gone need that twenty five grams or not," Phill asked? "Yeah we need it now," Double J said. "I can't get it for ya'll right now but I'll have somebody get it for ya'll later," Phill said.

"We gone have the g we owe you to when you sell us the twenty five grams, so we'll bring the whole four thousand with us," Slim said.

"I gotta go, I'll holla at ya'll later on," Phill said. "Make sure we get them twenty five grams today our joint is outta work," Slim said. "I got ya'll don't worry about it," Phill said. "A'ight we'll holla at you," Slim said.....

Later on that day they were sitting in Double J's crib chilling, when they got a call from Phill telling them that he was going to send his guy John over with the twenty five grams, and that they needed to make sure the four stacks was counted up right before they gave it to John.....

Once John delivered the twenty five grams they went straight to Doubles J's kitchen table and started bagging up.....

"How many pills we gone use," Double J asked? "We gone use three first to see how the dopefiends like it with three on it," Slim said.....

Both of them begin opening up the seventy five capsules and dumping the inside of the dorms on the table on top of the twenty five grams.....

"Lord if this dope is any good we finna be getting money like never before. Fuck spending our money we need to stack our shit, and get into some real estate, then we can leave the dope game alone," Slim said. "Yeah I agree with you on that. You know all these other niggas be spending their shit, then when it comes time for bound money they can't even bound out for ten or fifteen stacks," Double J said.....

As they continued mixing up the dope they both imagined of riches.....

They next day they put the dope on their joint, and to their surprise the dope fiends loved it.....

They finished that twenty five grams in one day, and was right back at Phill buying fifty grams this time. Phill was a player that liked to see niggas doing good getting money so he sold them fifty grams for fifty five hundred.....

Once they put that fifty grams out their they thought it would slow down some because the dopefiends would know from the last twenty five grams that they aint selling the same dope they had originally when they first opened up.....

Double J and Slim sat back at the end of the park admiring the veiw of the customers swarming to buy dope. It was as if everytime the pack worker would bring out a new pack the dopefiends would swarm on him like flies to shit.....

"How the hell is our joint tipping like this with Phill's dope, and his joint aint putting up numbers like ours," Double J asked? "That cuz Phill, and alot of these other niggas be putting that crazy shit on they dope, that's why I told you we aint gone use nothing but dorms. Phill nam still checking a bag but their turnover rate is slower," Slim said.....

Within a month Double J, and Slim was the men. Their joint was putting up numbers. They had bought new Cadillacs, new sports cars and all. Their team of workers constantly grew. Ho's coming from everywhere trying to get with them..... Throughout it all they continued to buy dope from Phill.....

CHAPTER 3

One hot sunny day Double J was simply bending blocks in the hood listening to Al Green puffing on joints that wasn't laced with cocaine when he seen her from the back in those jeans.....

Damn this ho thick as hell, Double J thought to himself.

He pulled up to her; once he seen her face he became disappointed. Aw this Cynthia dopefiend ass, he thought to himself.

Cynthia immediately opened the passenger side door and just jumped in his car.....

"Take me to your spot to get some dope," she said. "I got a few bags in my pocket," Double J said. "What are you doing riding around with dope in your pocket," Cynthia asked? "What else am I doing with dope in my pocket," Double J said sarcastically. "I didn't know you shoot dope," Cynthia said. "Tell somebody, and I'll kill you," Double J said.

They drove to a quiet block on the outskirts of the hood, pulled over and parked.

Double J gave Cynthia the dope to hook it up and put in the needle.

Once she hooked the dope up and put it in the needle she tried handing the needle to Double J.

"Naw you go ahead, ladies first," Double J said.....

With her right hand she shot dope into the veins of her left arm as her eyes rolled in the back of her head, as her entire body felt as if it was taken to a whole nother planet.

Afterwards she passed the needle to Double J.

With his right hand he shot dope into the veins of his left arm.

As Barry White song I'm never gone leave your love played on the radio Double J felt as if he was soaring above the clouds.....

Afterwards Double J dropped Cynthia off at home and went and met Slim at his crib to shake up some dope.....

"I bought a hundred grams instead of fifty," Slim said. "That's cool," Double J said.

"Start busting the dorms down I gotta go use the bathroom, my stomach fucked up from smoking all them lace joints," Slim said.....

Slim came out the bathroom and seen Double J sitting at the table nodding and scratching.

"Damn nigga you look like you done had a dope," Slim said. "Naw man I'm just sleepy," Double J said.

So they both begin busting the dorms down.

Double J kept scratching and nodding at the table.

This nigga fucking around with dope, Slim thought to himself.

"Lord tell the truth aint you getting high," Slim asked? "Nigga you know damn well I been getting high ever since you've known me," Double J said. "Nigga you know what I'm talking about is you fucking with dope," Slim said.....

Double J paused for a little while.....

"Yeah I fuck around with the dope a little," Double J said. "What made you turn into a dopefiend," Double J asked? "I use to be seeing how dopefiends look after they get high. Some of them looked like it's the best feeling in the world. Some of them be looking like they're walking on the clouds or some shit. Then I start to see how the dopefiends do whatever it takes to get money for dope, that made me want to try some even more, cuz I knew it had to be some good shit. Once I tried it, it felt like heaven on Earth. No lie, am a be a dopefiend forever. Am a get high til I die," Double J said.

Slim looked at Double J with a smirk on his face thinking to himself, this nigga done lost his mind.....

"Niggas always trying to belittle dopefiends, when they get high they motherfucking self off all type of shit. A drug addict is a drug addict. It don't matter if you smoke weed, lace weed, tut cocaine, tut dope, or shoot dope you still a drug addict," Double J said. "I can agree with you on that cuz I smoke more lace joints than some people use dope," Slim said.

"We gone have to start paying somebody to bag up this dope this shit a headache," Slim said. "Straight up," Double J said.....

Days to follow Slim begin to admire how suave Double J was as he was high off dope.

As he walked, talked, drove, ate, smoke cigarettes, and each and every way he maneuvered was super cool when he was drunk off dope.....

Before long Slim begin asking Double J a gang of questions on how it feels to be high off dope.....

"You steady asking me about how it feels to be high off dope. My best answer is you wont know how it feels until you try it," Double J said. "I'm scared of needles," Slim said. "You aint gotta shot it, you can tut it. But it aint nothing look shooting it, as that dope run up your veins, it's the best high you'll ever experience," Double J said.

Slim was still hesitant to try dope he let his pride get in the way, he knew certain people looked down on dopefiends.....

A couple days later at a club with these two lesbian chicks he dated and paid for sex he begin wanting to try some dope again.

The lesbian chicks Tricey, and Reese did it all, besides dope. They snorted lines of cocaine, smoked lace joints, regular weed, and smoked leaf.....

After downing a few drinks at the club. The girls sat at the table snorting line after line of cocaine, secretly not in the publics eye.

"Damn ya'll gone fuck around and O.D.," Slim said. "That's only if you use dope, you ain't gonna find to many people O.Deing off cocaine, although you can O.D. off cocaine," Reese said.

"Have ya'll ever fucked around with dope before," Slim asked? "Hell naw, we aint no motherfucking dopefiends," Tricey said. "Shiiit ya'll get high off every thing else," Slim said. "Everything besides dope," Tricey said.

"I heard that dope is the best high known to mankind," Slim said. "Yeah me to. But it takes control over your body, you gotta have it or your body wont be able to function right. And I heard the sickness is a motherfucker," Tricey said.

"I wanna snort a line or two to see how it feels," Slim said. "So you wanna be a dopefiend," Reese said sarcastically. "Naw I just wanna snort just one bag of dope to see how it feels. I want ya'll to snort it with me," Slim said. "Hell naw," Reese said. "Let's all three of us try it together," Slim said.....

For almost an hour at the club Slim tried convincing the girls to snort a bag of dope with him, and it worked.....

Slim pulled up to his dope spot.....

"Tyrone who working Lord," Slim asked? "Ush working," Tyrone said. "Why don't I see nobody shopping," Slim asked? "It's kinda slow right now, but you can best believe it'll be a gang of customers in line in no time," Tyrone said.

"Go get me three bags of dope, and hurry up Lord," Slim said.

Tyrone rushed to go get three bags from Ush, and brought it right back to the car..... Slim took the dope and smashed off.

Slim parked a few blocks over from his joint.....

He tore open a bag of dope with his teeth and laid it on one of the girls cigarette box. He tore a piece of the paper off his match box. He scooped up half the dope and snorted it like a pro.

He sat the Newport box on the dash and leaned back in his seat to feel the total effect of the dope.

Within seconds Slim had his door opened bent over throwing up his guts.

I'f that shit gone have me throwing up like that I don't even want none, Tricey thought to herself.

After Slim finished throwing up he snorted the other half of the dope off of the Newport box.

He laid back in his seat and relaxed for minutes and begun to feel the effect of being drunk off dope.

The girls then snorted their bags.

As they laid there high they all thought within their own silent minds that dope was the best drug known to men.....

Slim, and both women winded up in a motel room. Slim dick stayed on hard all the while. Slim had heard of the dope dick, but didn't know that it was this intense.....

For the entire week to follow Slim snorted dope, and smoked laced joints each day.

One morning as Slim went home he got into it with his main girlfriend. She was tired of him spending nights out, and cheating on her..... She through some hot coffee on him, and swung on him a few times leaving him with a few minor scars on his face..... Slim stormed out the house and went to his joint.....

Slim pulled on the joint got two bags of dope pulled around the corner to blow them.....

He pulled back around to his joint sat on the hood of his car smoking a lace joint, thinking of all the good times, and the bad times he had, had with his girlfriend..... He was still a little pissed off cuz she put her hands on him.....

Double J pulled of laughing.....

"So I see you having problems with your girl," Double J said. "How you know," Slim asked? "Cuz I see you sitting there faced all scratched up looking crazy, I know you aint let no nigga do it to you, because we'll be in war right now," Double J said.....

Slim tossed the duck of the joint on the ground, and bailed in with Double J, and Double J pulled off.....

"Man this ho crazy as soon as I walked through the door she got to throwing shit, hollering, screaming, and swinging," Slim said. "We all go through problems with women, that's been going on since the beginning of time," Double J said.....

"Pull over for a minute I need to take care of some business," Slim said.

Double J pulled over and put the car in park.

"What you gotta piss or something," Double J asked? "Naw I need to take care of something else," Slim said.

Slim pulled out his pack of cigarettes. Then pulled out a bag of dope, opened it with his teeth and poured it on the cigarette box..... Double J remained silent couldn't believe what he was seeing.

Slim then pulled out a small piece of a straw and snorted the entire bag of dope. Double J just sat there looking at him like he was crazy.

Slim fired up a cigarette, and looked at Double J and asked, "Is my nose clean." "Yes it's clean," Double J said.

"I can't believe you sat there and snorted a bag of dope after you been getting down on me after you found out I was getting high," Double J said. "I been seeing how good you been looking when you high off dope, it be like you be walking on clouds or some shit, and I wanted that feeling so I tried it, and I love it," Slim said. "I told you it was a bomb, especially if you shoot it," Double J said.....

Double J begin smiling and pulled off listening to Barry White's song Ecstasy, as they drove to the mall.....

Once they made it inside the mall Slim became so happy with seeing all the ho's there that he had forgot all about what him and his girl had went through earlier.....

Slim winded up getting a gang of numbers from ho's.

185

As they entiered this one shoe store Slim couldn't take his eyes of this white chick. She was raw as hell. She was about 5.6", 140 lbs., a red hed, with black eyeline around her red lipstick, with hazel blue eyes. She looked like a model or some shit.

Slim decided to walk over and strike up a conversation with her.....

Slim came to find out that her name was Angie, she lived on the north side of town. Twenty years of age with no boyfriend, no kids, or none of that. They exchanged numbers, and went their seperate ways.....

All the rest of the day Slim couldn't stop thinking of Angie she just looked so good to him.....

Slim went home that night, and made up with his girl, as they got down within break up to make up sex.....

Slim had never been with a white woman before but always wanted one..... The next day Slim winded up giving Angie a call, he thought she was gone be on some phony shit, but he was wrong she was real cool.....

Slim and Angie starting hanging out together damn near everyday..... One of the things Slim liked about Angie was that she genuinely liked him for him; she wasn't like the other women that he'd fucked around with, they was only interested in money one way or the other, Angie wasn't.....

Within a couple months Slim left his main girl for Angie, and moved in with her.....

Within several months Double J and Slim found there dope habits increasing. Having to spend more money to support their habits, for guns, money on bonding their guys outta jail, and started having to pay more bills. This fortune and fame wasn't all what it seemed.....

CHAPTER 4

"Roxanne you need a ride," Slim asked? "Naw no thank you, here come my bus now," Roxanne said. "Girl get in you aint gotta wait on no bus," Slim said. "No, it's okay, thanks anyway," Roxanne said. "Get in I insist," Slim said.....

She winded up getting in.....

She looked around the inside of his Cadillac and noticed that it was super clean. The upholstery looked as if it was brand new from the manufacturing place.....

He put on some Teddy Pendergrass, Turn off The Lights, as he pulled of she immediately made herself comfortable.

"Where do you need me to take you to," Slim asked? "I need you to drop me off at the Cook County hospital," she said. "Whats wrong with you," he asked? "Aint nothing wrong with me, I'm going to see my friend, she just had a baby," she said. "Do you have any kids," he asked? "I don't have no kids, nor a boyfriend," she said.....

Roxanne was one of Slims grammer school friends that he'd only see every once in a while..... On the rest of the short ride there they begin to reminisce about grammer school..... They both admitted that they had been liking each other since grammer school.....

As he pulled up in front of the hospital he tried to park.....

"Naw you aint gotta park. Just let me out in the front," she said. "You need me to come back and pick you up, when you get finished seeing your friend," he asked? "Naw I'm straight," she said. "What's up with later on let's go somewhere and fuck," Slim said as they both begin laughing. "Naw I'm just joking about fucking, but serious lets get together and kick it later on," he said.....

She reached into her purse and pulled out a little card with her phone number on it and handt it to him.....

"Well here go my number just call me later on tonight," she said.....

As she walked into the hospital Slim just sat there watching her in a daze imagining what she'd look like naked.....

Later on that day Slim called her as the phone rang seven times he didn't get any answer..... He called her three more times, periodically, but still didn't get no answer.

After calling her for the fifth time he finally got an answer.....

"Hello," she said. "Hello can I speak to Roxanne," Slim said. "Yes this is me," she said. "This Slim, let me come through and pick you up," he said. "Why you wait so late," she asked? "I been calling you all day, aint nobody answer the phone," he said. "I been running errands for my granny. I been in and out the house all day. You got bad timing, you must been calling the times when I was out. Fuck it come on over and pick me up we'll kick it for a little while," she said.....

He went over picked her up. They rode around seeing the sites and reminiscing for about thirty minutes. Then he took her back home.....

Days to follow he begin sneaking off from Angie to hang with Roxanne almost everyday for about two weeks straight. Each time they was together she refused to give the pussy up.....

One night Slim was drunk off dope, and liquor, and had been smoking lace joints. He had his mind set on fucking the shit outta Roxanne this particular night.

He went to her house unannounced. She got dressed and decided to kick it with him anyway.

As she entered his car she smelled the smoke from lace joints.....

"Why do you gotta smoke that stuff," she asked? "Cuz it makes me feel good, you need to try it," he said. "Never that, I'll never use drugs. I don't need drugs to make me feel good, I get high off life," she said.

"Getting high off life, I liked that, that sounded slick," he said.

As they cruised down the street listening to Al Greens, Let's Stay Together, both of them became relaxed. She begin slowly taking off her shoes to get comfortable.

Outta the corner of his eyes he looked at her admiring her beauty.

"Let's go somewhere and chill out," he said. "We already chilling out," she said. "Naw let's get a room or something," he said. "Hell naw, we aint getting no room or none of that until you get rid of her, and let me become your main girl," she said. "Who is her," he asked? "You know who she is the woman that you go home to every night when you drop me off. The one you share your love and life with, the one you live with," she said.....

He paused trying to think of some good game to pop back at her but couldn't because he knew she was speaking the truth.....

"But I been with her for a long time now and I just can't up and leave her," he said. "Well whenever you do decide to leave her I'm willing to fill in her position and take on all responsibilities. And when I say all responsibilities thats exactly what I mean," she said as she looked him in his eyes seductively.....

As he cruise the streets they peacefully listened to Al Green as thoughts of her in pornographic positions raced through his mind he'd visualize his dick in and out her pussy, ass, and mouth.....

He pulled up at a liquor store and parked.....

"Do you want me to get you something to drink," he asked? "A pink lemonade," she said.

As he exited the car thoughts of him, and her walking down the aisle getting married raced through her mind.

She really liked him but the only way he was going to get between her legs was if she was his main girl and only girl.

He came back into the car with two bottles of Champagne, two cups, the pink lemonade, and a few bags of chips.

He instantly popped open a bottle and poured some Champagne in a cup. Handt her the other cup.

"Naw I'm straight you know I don't drink," she said. "Try it out just for tonight, just for me," he asked? "Thanks but no thanks, I don't drink," she said.

She grabbed the pink lemonade opened it and begin sipping on it like it was the best lemonade she ever had, as they pulled off and begun cruising through the town.....

Roxanne reached into her purse and pulled out a pickle. She took the pickle out of it's wrapper and begin sucking on it like it was a dick. For a long time she pulled the pickle in and out her mouth sucking on it like she was trying to suck out all the juices from it.

Her reasoning for sucking on the pickle like that was to tease and entice him to wanna be with her and only her.

After cruising for a little while Slim pulled in this vacant lot right next to this body shop where he use to get his cars spray painted at. The shop was closed because it was so late at night.

As they begin listening to Stevie wonder's Ribbon In They Sky they started to reminiscing about past times, and began talking about things they'd like to do in the future..... Slim begin to roll a joint.

"Uhhhh, you aint finna smoke that while I'm in here," she bodly said. "Don't worry I aint gone lace it," he said. "It don't matter if you lace it or not, you aint finna smoke that while I'm in here," she said. "Am a crack the window," he said. "You gone have my clothes smelling like weed," she said. "I told you am a crack the window," he said. "Fuck it gone head," she said.

He finish rolling up the joint and sat fire to it. He inhaled and exhaled the smoke harshly, which instantly boosted his dope high.

This shit a bomb he thought to himself.

He begin to try to convince her for sex, she still wasn't interested.

After he finished the joint he downed a half bottle of Champagne.

As he was downing the Champagne he visualized her and him fucking, and sucking each other.

He begin rubbing on her titties.....

"Stop boy don't put you hands on my titties I aint no ho. I don't get down like that," she said.

He then grabbed her left tittie. She snatched his hand away from her titties.

"Drop me off, drop me off," she said.....

In a frustrating sex craving rage he locked his car doors, ripped off her shirt as she begin yelling, kicking, and screaming.

He upped a .38 outta his jacket pocket, and told her "bitch shut the fuck up". And she immediately shut the fuck up.

Tears begin to roll down her face as he snatched off the rest of her clothes, then her panties in a storming rage.

He forced her to bend over the front seat and swiftly unbutton his pants and pulled them down to his knees craving for her pussy.

He tried to force feed her pussy his dick but it didn't work because her pussy was to tight, his dick was to big to get in.

She continued silently crying and pleading inside her heart and mind for him to stop, but he didn't.

With the gun in his left hand he spat in his right hand and rubbed it on the tip of his dick for lubrication.

He worked on getting his dick in her pussy. After a minute the tip of his dick finally slipped in. As he slowly worked his dick in and out her pussy to get it wet he began thinking to himself, damn this ho pussy tight as hell.

Once her inner juices begin flowing within he commence to slamming his dick in and out her pussy in a furious rage as she continued crying.

To him it seemed as if every stroke her pussy got weter and weter.

After the eighth pump he put the gun in his jacket pocket, and squeezed her waist, stopped pumping, and held his dick in her pussy until his entire nut was released in her guts.

He took his dick out, and grabbed her by the shoulders and turned her body around to face him.

"Please, please, please stop," she cried out to him.

He back hand slapped her with his left hand.....

"Shut up Bitch," he said.

She did exactly what he said. He pulled the gun back outta his jacket and put it to her head.

"Bitch suck this dick," he said. "Please, please, don't do this," she cried out. "Bitch suck this dick before I kill you," he said.

She begin crying even harder and pouting like a little kid, as her life flashed before her eyes she wrapped her lips around his dick.

She begin to suck his dick like never before. The wetness of her mouth, combined with her deep throat, and his high made it feel so good that he instantly unleashed a globb of nut down her throat as she swallowed it all.....

"Bitch get in the back seat," he said. "Please, please let me leave," she cried out.

He slapped her busting her bottom lip. She jumped in the back seat frightened of what he'd do if she didn't do what he told her to do.

She got on the back seat face down crying, laying flat on her stomach as he begin raping her in the ass.

She'd never felt so much pain in her life. He never felt so much pleasure in his life.

As he begin nutting it was as he visualized the skies filled with fire works similar to the fourth of July.....

He pushed her outta the car, and threw her clothes on top of her.

He smashed off listening to I'm Never Gone Leave Your Love, by Barry White.

At that very moment Slim felt as if he ruled the world. He loved the power he achieved from raping her.....

As Roxanne sat in the lot scared to death putting on her clothes a car drove pass slowly.

It was two individuals in the car, an old lady and her daughter coming from church.....

"Mom it's a lady in that lot naked," the little girl said. "Hush up now it aint nobody in no lot naked," the old lady said. "It is, it is, we need to go back and help her," the little girl said.

Her mother looked at her and seen the sincerity in her words, and pulled over.

"Girl if you have me to go back and it's not a naked woman there lord knows what am a do to you when we get home," the old lady said.....

She made a u-turn and went back to see if there really was a naked woman. As she pulled up to the lot Roxanne ran to her car with no shoes or shirt on nothing but her skirt with her hands over her titties crying, "please help me, please help me".

She jumped into the back seat of the four door car.....

"Oh my God, what happen to you," the old lady said historically. "He raped me," Roxanne cried out in a loud voice.

The old lady immediately drove off. Her and her daughter was in shock, they'd never experience being in a situation like that before.

Nervous, scared, unfocused, and not being able to drive right the old lady told Roxanne we gotta get you some clothes and take you to the hospital, and report this to the police.

"No, no police," Roxanne said with authority.

Roxanne didn't wanna get the police involved cuz she knew Slim was a ViceLord, and she knew what ViceLords would do to her if they found out she told the police on one of their members.....

"Please just take me home," Roxanne said frantically. "You sure you don't want me to take you to my home and get you cleaned up first," the old lady asked? "Naw please just take me home," Roxanne said. "Where do you live," the old lady asked?

Roxanne gave her, her address.

The rest of the ride all three of their minds was filled with sick satanic thoughts, as each individual remained silent.....

Once the old lady pulled up in front of Roxanne's house she looked at her feeling sorry and sad for her.....

"You sure you'll be okay," the old lady ask? "I'm going to be alright," Roxanne said with tears running down her face.....

Roxanne got out the car with her hands over her breast running to her door step. She rung the doorbell twice then her grandmother let her in as she feel to floor crying out, "he raped me".....

The old lady and her daughter rode home crying, and mentally thanking God that they'd never been attacked or raped before.....

Roxanne's grandmother and the rest of the family pleaded with her to tell the cops but she never did. Roxanne didn't want to jeopardize the safety of herself and her family.....

A couple days later Roxanne's family sent her to live in Atlanta with her aunt Rachel.....

A few days later Phill pulled up to Slim and Double J's joint, and parked in the middle of the street, and bailed outta the car.....

"Yous a stupid motherfucker, you done went and raped that girl. Do you know how much time rapes carry. Nigga aint no ViceLord gotta rap no ho's. Shiit we got ho's throwing us the pussy," Phill said, as he ran back to his car and smashed off burning rubber.....

Double J looked at slim with a frown on his face with curiousity running through his head.

"Man what the fuck is Phill talking about," Double J asked? "I don't know what that nigga tripping about," Slim said. "What the fuck he talking about somebody got raped," Double J said. "I told you I don't know what the fuck that nigga talking about," Slim said.

Later on that day Phill came through and politely closed Double J and Slim down. He took their joint and gave it to one of the universal elites. Phill was tired of Double J and Slim bullshit. They wasn't paying him his g a week. They was leaving their workers in jail wasn't bonding them out. Nor was they standing on nation business. Then, and then this nigga Slim went and raped a ho.....

Phill found out about the rape through Roxanne's lil cousins that was Renegade ViceLords. Roxanne's cousins was shorties, they wasn't experienced in gun slanging yet, so they hollered at Phill to see if Phill would violate Slim. Phill lied and told them he'd violate them if they made sure she didn't press charges..... Roxanne never press charges.....

Now Slim and Double J didn't have a joint to sell their dope on; Slim was mad at Double J for the money he fucked up in the past. Double J was mad at Slim for commiting that rape. Both of them was mad at Phill for taking their joint.

Slim and Double J didn't talk to each other for almost a week.

Slim ended up going over Double J's crib to get back some of his belongings.

Double J and Slim ended up making back up.

They went to this dope spot on the low end that suppose to had some good dope.....

For the first time in life Slim shot dope into his veins. The rush felt better than sex, snorting dope, smoking lace joints, or any other thing he'd experienced in life..... From that day forth Slim felt the true meaning of high til I die, because Slim knew he'd forever be a dopefiend.....

CHAPTER 5

Months later, January, 1972

Slim and Double J had become straight up dopefiends. Majority of their cars was confiscated by the repo man. All their jewelry, leathers, and almost everything else they owned were sold or either pawn.

They had been accustom to making fast money, and spending it fast; they had an expensive cost of living. But by them steady spending fast, and not making it fast no more the money the did possess started to become extinct......

They had resorted to doing whatever it took to get high; they was on some straight dope fiend shit.

Slim had begun doing a little pimping to get money to buy dope. Double J was against soliciting women.

Although Double J was true dopefiend he still respected women.

One night Double J and Slim had finished doing some petty hustling. Double J decided to spend a night at Slim's crib, Double J usually didn't spend nights out, he'd go home to his wife each night, but not this night.....

The next morning Double J woke up outta his sleep as the sun shined on his face.

Double J went into the bathroom to take a piss, and then went to Slim's room with one thing on his mind, getting some dope.

As he walked to Slim's bedroom he noticed that the bedroom door was partially opened. He didn't want to knock just in case they were asleep. So he looked in it to see if they were woke; and yes they were wide awoke.....

To Double J surprise there were Slim, Slim's white chick Angie, and two black women Reese and Tricey.....

There Slim stood with his shirt off, face and head looking like he aint shaved in years nodding, and shooting dope into his veins.

The three women was on the bed doing the nasty..... Angie was on all fours while Reese tortured her pussy from the back with this big black strap on dildo, as Tricey was on her knees holding Angie head to her pussy. It was as she was forcing her to eat her pussy.

"Bitch stop acting like you aint up with it and perform for the customers," Slim said.

Slim had turned innocent Angie out to a drug fiend, and a prostitute.

Double J bust in the room.

"Lord, what the fuck is you on. You done turned your main girl into a ho," Double J said. "Shes my bottom bitch," Slim said. "But that damn girl is four months pregnant, and you got her selling pussy to other women," Double J said.

The three ladies kept doing what they was doing, as if Slim or Double J wasn't even there.

"Nigga do you want to fuck her," Slim asked? "Naw man you know I'm married, but let me get some of that dope," Double J said.

Slim gave Double J the needle as he watched the girls sexing he shot dope into his veins.....

Chapter samples of previously published
Urban Fiction Novels by Alan Hines

Lost in a Poet Storm

CHAPTER 1

"Stop hitting on me, Randell stop hitting on me," Thunder said as Randell continued slapping her around.....

Randell slapped her to the floor pulled down her jogging pants upped his dick, and started fucking her in the ass as she screamed, and yelled because of the tormenting pain.....

"Randell stop fucking me in my ass, stop fucking me in my ass, stop fucking me in my ass," she said in a screeching voice. As she continued to cry out, and plead for him to stop he didn't listen.....

Thunder screams awoke her daughter Neese up. Neese jumped out her bed ran to see what was going on with her mom. As she made it to the bedroom she seen her mom stretched out as Randell held her down slamming his dick off in her ass.

207

Randell nutted in her ass, and let her up. She jumped up crying.

"Aww naw you just fucked me in my ass, you fucked me in my ass, you fucked me in my ass," Thunder said.

Randell looked at his rock-hard dick. I wanna do it again, he thought to himself....

Thunder looked at her bedroom door, and seen Neese standing there....

"Neese, baby go to your room, and close the door," Thunder said.

Neese didn't move didn't want to leave her mom in distress....

"Neese, baby please go to your room everything is okay, I'll be there in a little while," Thunder said while whipping tears from her own eyes....

This time Neese listened. She walked back to her room laid in her bed, and put the cover over her head....

I hate that stud, Neese said to herself....

From that day forth Neese promised herself that she'd never let a man put his hands on her or disrespect her in any shape form or fashion....

Every time Neese would turn around Randell would violently domestically annihilate her mom....

In the back of Neese's young mind she wish the bitch Randell would literally die, and that her father was still living....

Although Neese's real father was killed when she was younger she'd still have constant pleasurable memories of him....

Neese's dad was a gang chief king of the Traveler ViceLords....

Each day after he was killed Neese would have these fond memories of all the long walks they'd have as her dad would talk her ears off implanting knowledge within her young mind so that in time she'd prevail to be a productive lady.....

"Sweetheart you must never eat pork, never poison your body with things that's no good for you," Will said. "Why daddy, why shouldn't I eat pork," Neese said to her father, in her mind as she reminisced to herself about her father. "In the Koran Allah father of the universe teaches us that his children are forbidden to eat Swine. The pig is one the most nastiest animal that exist. The pig consumes all types of nasty food to eat then those that eat the pig in turns will eat all the things the pig has ate. For those that eat pig will in turn find themselves in an early grave because of all the disease he has to offer to mankind." Will said....

"Sweetheart I know you're only a little girl, and I may talk you to death, but I'm giving you these timeless jewels to help you get through life. Life is what you make it and you're going to make the best out of your life," Phill said....

"Once you get older and you start dating, you make sure the love and respect is mutual. Never let your boyfriend put his hands on you, the first time he put his hands on you, your relationship should be over," Phill said.

"In life never sit back and wait on a Welfare check get up make moves. When and if you finish college that will be great, but my advice to you is to go to college so you can be your own boss, not working for someone's company and being called a boss. A lot of people got the word boss misunderstood; boss is when you are the owner or part owner a boss is not a supervisor or a manager. I know you're going to pick your own major when and if you do go to college, but consider studying law to be a lawyer. Lawyers are their own bosses, because they have their own law firm, and lawyers are respected even by the racist police, don't nobody want no trouble out of lawyers, not even politicians....

As Phill continued to hold his only child Nesse's hand walking her to school, as she looked up at her dad, and towards the sunlight as he kept talking to her about being productive in life, she didn't understand some of the things he was talking about, but listen attentively.....

CHAPTER 2

At an early age when Neese was only six years of age her dad was killed. Bullets ripped through his flesh separating life and death....

As years progressed along, she'd miss her dad more and more. Her dad was like her best friend, and a father mixed in one.

As the years continued to move on she would still have visions of her walking holding her dad's hand looking up at him, and up at the sun while he would feed her brain knowledge....

As a kid when it started to thunder and rain Neese would always run outside in the rain, she loved the rain. Sometimes after it rain, she would try to find a Rainbow to follow it so she could try to find the pot of gold after the Rainbow.

She loved the rain so much her mother nicknamed her Storm.

Although her dad was gone, and she was so young she'd still follow his guidelines. She maintained the best grades all through school. She'd get her class work done so fast that she would sit in class and write down on a piece of paper. It started as thoughts and turned into rhymes which later turned into poetry.

A few times once she was done the teacher wondered what she wrote down, the teacher went over to read the paper come to find out it was poetry in which the teacher liked. Later the teacher had Storm to read one of her poems in front of the class; Storm thought the class would clown her, but contrary to her beliefs the class loved it....

All throughout grammar school Nesse stayed on the honor roll and in the gifted class....

Freshmen year in high school was a blast. She went to an all-girl school she noticed that the girls had always been jealous of her, so she stayed to herself. She maintained friends that didn't go to her school....

As years overlapped it was Storms senior year. The girls started spreading bogus rumors, about her being a lesbian and seeing her at a gay club and walking down the street holding hands with another woman, which wasn't true. Storm was a virgin would never even consider having sex with another woman, never even had sex with a man before. It went back to her youth as she'd look up to her dad, and the sun at the same time how he'd preach to her about being against homosexuality in which Storm was against. Storm investigated to see who was spreading bogus rumors. She found the girl who said it, and asked her if she said it, she said yes, she said it. Before Storm knew it, she had laid hands on her, and they was pulling each other hair and exchanging punches. The girl got the best of Storm, Storm pissed on herself. Days after the fight Storm was the talk of the town, she got her ass whopped and pissed on herself. Storm, and the girl she was fighting got suspended for a week. Storm never went back to embarrassed. She transferred to another school to finish the rest of the Senior year....

In time that small rumor of her being gay would haunt her mind for years to come....

After high school she took only on-line college courses. She wanted to study law like her father wanted her to but instead decided to take two different majors, math and computer science.

More, and more guys would be at her wanting to fuck, but she remained a virgin, she wasn't even willing to have a boyfriend until later on in the futuristic time of life.

She'd see her mom Thunder a crack head; it was like seeing the burning of eternal fire in the form of flesh. Throughout it all she always respected her mother no matter what, she loved her mom; she knew if her dad was still living her mom would've never turned into a drug addict. Her mom started getting high shortly after her dad was killed; to ease the pain of no longer having him there. In turns her mom met a deadbeat boyfriend that was a drug addict as well that use to punch her and beat her. As a kid Storm wished her mother's boyfriend would just die....

Storm lived in the hood she'd roam the streets sometimes as a way of being free. Each time she'd pass the dope spots in the hood the guys would always try to get with her, she always denied them she didn't want no street nigga. All the time she'd roam the streets in the hood she'd hear many of the guys putting issues on King Phill constantly, to her that was so immature, and sounded like the repeating of a broken record.

Storm had heard about the poetry clubs but never been not even once but yearned for the day she could flex her skills on the open mic.

One day she visited the poetry club for an audition and to her surprise after the audition

they told her she'd be hitting the open mic in a few days. The poem she recited at the audition was called my father's name: My father's name in vain so they glorify off fame.

Distribution for currency exchange hustling passing time
as it's a game. By law we were supposed to uplift and safeguard our community enhance gain.
Love life through the creators will to gain.
The love the life the loyalty, in its entirety everything.

The days that exchanged for moonlight nights in which a few of them passed and she was ready to hit the mic for the first time. She went backstage to meet the other poets, as smoke lingered in the room each poet was in their own zone, somewhere quiet in deep thought, while others was reciting poetry at a low tone....

Storm recognized this guy from her hood. His nickname and poet name were the same. He went by the nickname Tears. People gave him that name because as a kid his eyes use to shed tears for no giving reason. Later in life Tears felt that the tears he was shedding was because of the heartache and tears him, and other people would be shedding over the years....

Storm approached Tears....

"Hey man I never knew you did poetry," Storm told Tears. "I never knew you did poetry either," Tears told Storm....

Tears told Storm his story on how he went to jail served 15 years straight for a body and that's how he started writing poetry....

Tears caught a murder for the nation in return the nation showed no love a lesson learn. So tears had it in his mind that when he'd touch the streets again he'd never sell dope or do anything else to risk his freedom.

Tears would get paid a few hundred dollars every week from the poetry club. Tears didn't want to sell drugs or be humping at a factory so although he only made a few hundred a week it was still good for him....

All the poets got together for prayer.

Following prayer Tears was first on the mic. He recited a poem called: Flashback.

Flashbacks of mishaps lives that was confiscated wont be coming back, stuck in a institutionalized system and wont be getting back, no letters, no money orders to keep ones on track. Love that disappeared was never all that. Crisis those crying out to the Lord to get they life back, tougher laws but didn't stop or slow down the killings they just got even more hideous reckless off track. Visions of those stuck in a maze of undying cravings of controlled substances in which they'll have until death becomes, until they die. Blood stains of tears that flow freely from ones eyes seeing the ancient black lives inhumane like animals in time, sad to see black on black crime.

Storm loved the poem it reminded her of something she would write herself. The second poet was named Lonnie Love, his real name was Lonnie, but he added the Love part to it because he writes mainly love poetry. Lonnie Love recited a poem called Nest: My hatched love from Nest, love of lifetime.

Mrs. Valentine.
Holy Divine.
Make love to my mind.
My sunshine.
My dream of love of life,
within lifetime.

Afterwards the audience stood up cheering and clapping....

The third poet was called Suicide. Just like all the other poets Suicide had a story to tell. Her story was that she was adopted as a child she never knew her real family and her adopted mother and father whom raised and loved her since she was a kid got killed in terrible car accident, she was left all alone is the cold world of frost circumstances. She named herself Suicide because she would constantly have thoughts of Suicide. Suicide first poem was called: Stained Mirror....

It was a stain in the mirror,
but yet and still she could see things clearer.
No Pilgrims or Happy Thanksgiving,
but instead roaches that fell from ceilings.
Gun shots of killings.
Abandon building living.
Mice that walked around as if they rented.
Kris Kringle ponded gifts on Christmas.
She'd bare witness to those that got high
as the only way to achieve a wonderful prism.
Over packed prisons of those that didn't listen
didn't abide by the fundamental written
guidance of the literature.
She'd seen those before her that made wrong
decisions, she'd let that be a lesson learned
off others failed missions.
Those that's telling the ones secretly planted
kisses.

Obituaries of those we love R.I.P. we miss them.
Lives that was confiscated over foolish and
petty issues.
She blanked out and broke all mirrors, more
then seven years bad luck superstition would
definitely continue.
Took a piece of the broken mirror and slide
both of her wrist tissue,
couldn't live the life of reality of a stain
mirror.

It was Storm's first time on the mic, she was
nervous. Suicide gave her a pep talk told her to not to
be scared but instead try to imagine if they wasn't there
as if she was home alone.

Storm stepped to the mic scared to death she tried
to use the method that Suicide told her, but it didn't
work. Storm had a poem memorized but couldn't get it
out so she just freestyled: Lady liberty.

Lady light.
Free us from bondages of life.
Give us new life.
Never ignorant getting goals accomplished, in
life.
Paradise.
Delight.
The things I like.
The soothing words of poetry I write.

The breezing through times,
the days of our lives.

Lady liberty.
Lady light.
Give us a sign of the time
a visionary of sight.

Lady liberty.
Lady light.

Everyone liked Storms poetry, her poetry was deep....

After the poetry club was over that night Storm went home and seen her mom eyes wide open foaming at the mouth, as if she had become part of the lifeless. Storm panicked and ran over to her shaking her saying her name back to back.

"I'm good stomach aching," Storm's mom Thunder said.

Storm looked at her mom's head seen it was nappy, looked at the thinness of her body brought back memories of when her mom was young and beautiful when her dad was still living before the drugs conquered her mom's existence. Storm could slightly smell the aroma of her mom's pussy, and knew she'd been out selling pussy. Storm loved her mom to death but hated seeing her mom as a drug fiend....

Once Suicide made it home in which she lived all alone, once again she wanted to commit Suicide. She looked at the window and just wanted to jump head first. She went into the bathroom looking in a stained mirror just like in her poem. While looking in the mirror in a split second she admired her own beauty while still living, as she could see herself lying dead inside a casket. With no second guess she grabbed a bottle of pills and took all 18 of them. Within moments of time she passed out on the bathroom floor. To only wake up the next day still living, such a disappointment for her....

The poetry club was only open three days a week Thursday, Friday, Saturday. Storm made a showing to recite pieces of poetry each time it was open. She began to question the owner of the club about why she wasn't getting paid when the other poets was getting paid. The owner told her it goes off request, once the audience start requesting her she would start getting paid....

Once weeks passed along the audience begin to request Storm more and more, started getting paid. Her pay was only several hundred a week, which was good for her because she lived with her family, Storm quit her job at the Supermarket and just survived off the money she was making from the poetry club.

Coincidently one night while at the club it rained outside. Tears would look out the window drowning in sorrow wishing for a better day tomorrow. Storm went over to talk to Tears, come to find out they had one thing main thing in common they both love the rain. Ever since he was a kid Tears always believe that when it rained that God was crying tears, that the raindrops were God's teardrops, because of the madness and sins his children would commit non-stop. Storm told Tears that she loved the rain, she even loved going out and getting wet in the rain, she told Tears that's how she got her name Storm....

At all times when Storm would hear gun shots, she lived in the hood so it was so common to her, but she despised that the gun shots came from Travelers against Travelers, the Travelers off the Double Up, was waring with the Travelers off Albany. Storm knew if her dad was still living there was no way ViceLords would be waring with one another, especially the Travelers that was her dad's very own branch of ViceLord....

CHAPTER 3

"Give a round of applause for poet Suicide," The announcer at the club said, as Suicide got on the mic, and blanked out reciting her poem she wrote titled Mental Disaster: Mental pics of my own self lying dead in a casket. killed by a teenager that had no father, no parental guidance, he was a dirty bastard.

Mental Pics of me being a slave, and having to call another human being master, what a disaster.
Mental pics of me being in the midst of the dragon, the beast empire doing sinful works being yelled at to do it faster.
Mental pics of me being stuck in a mental institution, seeing illusions, confusions.
A prison of disaster, everlasting.

Souls that shall get eternal life in hell,
burn in eternal fire.
Drugs that took people higher.
A socialism of Pinocchio's liars and evilness of
preaching pastors....
Mental images of disaster.

Next to the mic was Tears, Tears recited a poem:

Caught in a whirlwind bloody teary eyes of
maze. Kidnapping our black sisters same as
ancient African slave trades. Land of Sodom
and Gomorrah rainbow parades, newborns
born with H.I.V. virus around the time they
reach an adolescent full blown A.I.D.S. In Jesus
name I pray for better days. Those wrongfully
convicted natural life on bunks in cells they
shall lay. Teenagers straight killers that will take
your life away. Bloody holidays. This is the land
the lives God made; Lucifer sick self-leading the
troops astray....

Next to the mic was Father Time: Time could
never rewind. If only we had the powers to turn back
the hands of time. Give a sight, a vision to the blind,
leading the blind. Live righteously, holy and divine.
Great things seek and find. Get through troublesome
times. Prepare right now for in the future we shall
overcome, we shall shine. In due time what was in the

dark shall come to light to shine, we shall overcome we shall be considered divine.

Next to the mic was Sight: I've seen those living breathing to those in caskets dead. Joy and happiness, days of stress upon head. Seen those free, and those confined away, calendars to shred. Seen those that was rich, same ones poor, and mislead. Seen those that was thought to be good but was snakes instead. Seen my only love I ever had turned out to be a lesbian in bed......

CHAPTER 4

"Mom want you stop drinking the doctors been told you that you won't live long if you keep drinking," Tears told his mom. "Fuck you, who is you to tell me stop drinking I don't say nothing we ya'll smoke ya'll weed and pop pills all day," Tears mom said. "But me smoking weed ain't life threatening," Tears said....

Tears went back and forth arguing with his mom about how she should stop drinking. She had just left the hospital body failure from drinking, she went straight from the hospital to the liquor store....

The doctor had told her years ago that if she keeps drinking she wont live very long.....

It was hard for her to stop drinking, liquor was her life, and would mentally take her away from this cold world we lived in.

Tears loved his mom dearly. Tears would remember the times when he was locked up trapped in a time frame stuck in the belly of the beast, where love from the homies the nation of ViceLord was deceased. His mom was his only love, only peace. If he didn't have his mom there would've been no money, no visits, no letters of love in existence. Over time everybody broke bad on him even his own family which was sad....

When times when he was feeling mental distortion, he'd go talk to his auntie Louise. Louise was an ex crack head that stop getting high and gave her life to the Lord.

When Louise did get high, she'd drift to a world of reality as it seems she speak her mind as a black queen. A lot of people didn't like being around her when she was high because they say she'd talk too much. But Tears loved it because she'd speak the truth.

When Louise did get high sometimes, she'd like to smoke in the closet. The first time Tears caught Louise smoking in the closet, he just yelled out, "you a closet smoker," as they both begin laughing.

Previous in life when Louise would take a blast of the missile filled with rock cocaine, as she'd speak her mind as it remains.

She'd take her mouth of the missile and began; "what the Italians did in the past black people doing in today but just on a different level of drug dealer they were more organized than blacks. No matter how laws change, people, places and things change drug dealings will never stop because people gone always get high," Louise said.

She'd take another hit off the missile inhaling, and exhaling the smoke; "I heard your cousin caught a drug case, I had a case one time just shopping for a few bags and the police caught me right after I purchased the bags. It was chaotic I couldn't speak up to defend myself everybody including my public defender was white, you just sit back and roll with the flow, they should at least allow you to say a little something to defend yourself but they don't, for all they know the police could've planted those drugs on me," Louise said.....

Tears snapped back to his current day and age as he ceased to contemplate of Louise former life when she was an addicted.

Tears begin to talk to Louise about his mom's drinking problem, that would someday make her fatal if she didn't stop. Louise told him is nothing he could do but leave it in God's hand and continue to pray....

The next night in the poetry club Tears was first on the mic:

"A never ending saga consumptions of alcohol and drug usage as a way of feeling a wonderful prism, from life from a distance problems, non-existence. Some will even pond the kids gift at Christmas. Please stop drinking. Love life to be increasing. We need you down here on Earth as an angelic creature."

The next poet to the mic was Lonnie Love: "She open my eyes to the sight of her rise. I'd visualize family ties, mom's apple pie, Heaven in the sky, babies that will never even cry. Legitimate reasoning why. An angel descending on Earth in my eyes. No surprise, flawless images of her in my eyes. No foolish pride. No games being utilize.

She opened my eyes to love that seem to be cast from the skies. Gave me sight as I was once blind. A love affair that I could never find. Intellect of a female version of Albert Einstein.

She opened my eyes to what the creator had design; what I was put on Earth to mastermind; to be all I can be and shine until the end of time.

She opened my eyes to the true love in her heart that was enshrined.

She opened my eyes to this love for her kind.

She opened my eyes.

The next poet was Suicide: Drowning in time.

Drowning in my own blood.
The completion of lifelines.
No happy Valentine's.
This little light of mine I'm gonna let
it shine.
Blind leading blind.
Civilizations decline.
This is your brain on drugs
as the eggs continue frying.

Once Suicide left the club, she had constant visions of Suicide as usual. Once she made it home, she stared in the stained mirror in her bathroom wishing she could die.

She grabbed a razor contemplated on sliding her risk but didn't want to feel such pain. She sat the razor down and went looking out her project window, wanted to take to the sky and fly before she'd die, but didn't have the courage....

CHAPTER 5

One night as Storm entered the back of the club as usual, she came in contact with the midst of smoke as all the poets were in the own zone. Some would be recited poetry to themselves at a low tone, others would be writing down poetry, while others would simply be brain storming.

Storm stepped to Tears as the begin a deep and meaningful conversation. While talking to Tears Storm noticed it was a few new poets; in the back of her mind she couldn't wait to her them rock the mic, Storm was hungry to hear poetry, craving as an appetite as a since of delight, sky rockets in flight.....

While talking to Tears she noticed this guy from her hood named Lil Wayne. She had always had a secret crush on him when she was a kid, but he was too old for her, he was about ten years older than her.

She stepped away from Tears and went to talk to Lil Wayne, she thought he didn't remember her, but he remembered her very well, although he hadn't seen her since she was a little girl. At this point in time although he was ten years older than her it didn't matter because they were both adults.

Storm came to find out just as Tears Lil Wayne started writing poetry while he was in the joint. Lil Wayne poetry name was Sidney; he gave himself that nickname because as he'd felt like when he recited his poetry he wanted to act out like Sidney Poitier.

Lil Wayne was a player he could talk ho's into doing the things for him that they wouldn't normally do for other guys. As she'd conversate with him freely of things in life as a visionary to see, the blossoming of eternal seeds of eternity, she felt free as can be. As Lil Wayne laid his mac down, she'd look into his low red eyes as he was high off smoking loud as a free enterprise. She began rubbing on his back as he'd spit game like a ancient pimp that had his eyes on the prize....

Eventually Lil Wayne, and Storm begin hanging out. Lil Wayne treated her like a queen. Storm was shocked that Lil Wayne never tried to have sex with her. What she didn't know that Lil Wayne would never try to have sex with her, he would just continue to mess around with her until she was ready, he knew she was a virgin and if he ever got the pussy he would have her on lock.

Lil Wayne would spend lots of money on her, take her places she never been before. Lil Wayne even hooked her up to do some shows here and there with some of the underground rappers he knew; she was even featured reciting poetry on a few of their songs, which was good all the way around the board, quick ways to make some extra cash.

After many months of Storm, and Lil Wayne being together he didn't even have to ask Storm wanted to give him the pussy. Her virgin body was calling for him to serve and protect it.

As their tongues tasted the sweetness of each others mouth, as they embarked into erotica. He swiftly took off her shirt and bra sucking the titties as if he was breast feeding. Pants and panties to the floor as his mouth connected to her pearl tongue, she was sprung. He turned around and ate her ass to her it was such a dynamic blast.

Now it was time for the moment of truth as he Vaseline his dick down it took him some time to enter, but once he did the hollering and scratches on his back overlapped....

He wanted to taste her Vagina lips once again, he wanted to taste her soul as pleasure would come to be as pleasures would unfold....